AN ANTHOLOGY OF
DOCTORAL WRITERS

VOLUME II

Research Methodology

SECOND EDITION

Foreword by Dr. Rich Schuttler

Edited by **Dr. Cheryl A. Lentz**

THE REFRACTIVE THINKER® PRESS

The Refractive Thinker®: An Anthology of Higher Learning
Volume II: Research Methodology, 2nd Edition

The Refractive Thinker® Press
9065 Big Plantation Avenue
Las Vegas, NV 89143-5440   USA

info@refractivethinker.com
www.refractivethinker.com

Books are available through The Refractive Thinker® Press at special discounts for bulk purchases for the purpose of sales promotion, seminar attendance, or educational purposes. Special volumes can be created for specific purposes and to organizational specifications. Please contact us for further details.

Orders placed on www.refractivethinker.com for students and military receive a 15% discount.

Copyright © 2011 by The Refractive Thinker® Press
Managing Editor: Dr. Cheryl A. Lentz

Library of Congress Control Number: 2011929140

Volume ISBNs: Soft Cover   978-0-9828740-6-6
                 E-book/PDF   978-0-9828740-7-3
*Kindle and electronic version available.

Refractive Thinker® logo by Joey Root, The Refractive Thinker® Press logo design by Jacqueline Teng, cover design by Peri Poloni-Gabriel, Knockout Design, www.knockoutbooks.com, final production by Gary A. Rosenberg, www.garyarosenberg.com.

Printed in the United States of America

10   9   8   7   6   5   4   3   2   1

Contents

QUALITATIVE

PHENOMENOLOGY

MIXED METHOD

"Research is to see what everyone else has seen, and to think what nobody else has thought."

—ALBERT SZENT-GYORGYI

Foreword

A s an educator and consultant, I have spent considerable years and energy helping people and organizations to achieve their full potential by helping them to see what they could not on their own. I do this by providing different *lenses* to refocus their assumptions, beliefs, perceptions, and values. The different lenses provide for insights than one cannot usually see without such mentoring.

For many, I believe critical thinking is unfortunately referred to as formalized thought processes that are not easy to understand. Yet we have been critically thinking since we were born. And, like any other skill, some people are better at it than others. The authors contributing to this volume are some of the best critical thinkers in their field of study and at what they do. They own the space where they work. We can all learn much from them if we open ourselves to the possibility.

Thinking outside the proverbial box is a common term by many for an entrepreneurial perspective; yet I believe that is flawed thinking. The true entrepreneur does not even consider a box. No matter what happens outside the box, one still has a reference to the box and thus one tends to get only incremental gains instead of breakthrough strategies. Refractive thinking, as offered in the anthologies, lets go of the box and provides thinking that *bends* in new and exciting ways.

I have long contended that 'common sense is not so common' thus the need to reflect, remember, learn, and relearn the basics of life, love, and work. How many times do we need to 'touch the hot stove' to realize we will burn ourselves by doing so?! The application of metaphors and analogies, as learning tools, help one to see one thing in terms or in relationship to another and often provides a story that is easily related to by others. For the open-hearted reader, let the authors here take you on their journeys of excited focus while producing a future that can make for a better world.

As each subject matter expert offers his or her exploration, you will sense the *bending* of thought and perspective much as light refracts moving from one medium to another. As the authors allude to their process, you will notice a sound and systematic approach to an exploration; much like early pioneers in any country who went out on their journeys to see what there was to see and then to share their findings with others. The context provided within suggests refractive thinking examples in business, healthcare, education, and other industries that contribute to a developing world society.

Refractive thinking begins to help us better understand how to move beyond current business models to how to solve the complex problems of tomorrow. This volume brings some of industry's best minds together who have developed a skill that many others have not yet—refractive thinking. Let us continue to learn from the masters and those who are here to challenge the world to rise above what is in place today.

Richard Schuttler, Ph.D.
Chief Operations Officer, Powerteam International
Author of *Laws of Communication: The Intersection Where Leadership Meets Employee Performance*

Preface

I *think* therefore I am.

—RENEE DESCARTES

I *critically think* to be.
I *refractively think* to change the world.

Welcome to *The Refractive Thinker®: Volume II:*
Research Methodology, 2nd Edition.

Thank you for joining us for the Spring 2011 edition, as we continue to celebrate the accomplishments of doctoral educators affiliated with many phenomenal institutions of higher learning. The purpose of this offering within the anthology series is to share another glimpse into the scholarly works of these participating authors, specifically on the topic of research methodology. Our goal is to add to our first edition of Volume II with additional unique and innovative applications of research methodologies. The purpose is to provide a resource that is beyond the conventional boundaries of textbook, providing individual chapters that students and faculty might consider with regard to doctoral dissertation.

This peer-reviewed resource offers a framework that presents key categories of research to include case study, ethnography, qualitative, phenomenology, mixed method, and quantitative—all which are unique. Further, these approaches reflect the construct of the refractive thinker where each author challenged the conventional wisdom and expanded beyond the traditional boundaries.

These authors dared to not just think outside of the box. Instead the box continues to evolve into exploring nearly entirely new ideas for construction of 'the box,' i.e., applicable methodology.

In addition to exploring various aspects of innovation, the purpose of *The Refractive Thinker*® is to serve the tenets of leadership. This is not simply a concept outside of the self, but comes from within, defining our very essence. The search becomes both a personal journey and a not yet finite destination.

The Refractive Thinker® is an intimate expression of who we are—the ability to think beyond the traditional boundaries of thinking and critical thinking. Instead of mere reflection and evaluation, one challenges the very boundaries of the constructs itself. If thinking is *inside* the box, and critical thinking is *outside* the box, we add the next step of refractive thinking, *beyond* the box. Perhaps the need exists to dissolve the box completely. As in our first five volumes, the authors within these pages are on a mission to change the world. They are never satisfied or quite content with *what is* or asking *why;* instead these authors intentionally strive to push and test the limits to ask *why not.*

Join us on this next adventure of *The Refractive Thinker*® where this edition of Volume II continues the discussion begun several years ago. This prior work included The Delphi Primer, as well as sections that included: mixed methods, qualitative, quantitative, and Research as Art. Remember not only do we offer two volumes for your consideration for your doctoral studies and research choices, but 20 individual e-chapters are also available should you desire to only select your favorites.

We look forward to your interest in discussing future opportunities. Let this collection of authors continue our journey which began with volume I. Come join us in our quest to be refractive thinkers and add your wisdom to the collective. We look forward to your stories.

Acknowledgments

The foundation of leadership embraces the art of asking questions—to validate and affirm *what* we do and *why*. Leaders often challenge this status quo, to offer alternatives and new directions, to dare to try something that has not yet been done as again proved true in this case with our second edition of Volume II. This publication required the continued leap of faith and belief in this new publishing model by those willing to continue forward on this voyage. As a result, please let me express my gratitude for the help of the many that made this project possible.

First, let me offer a special thank you to Trish Hladek for her unwavering support and belief that traversing unchartered waters is worthy of the journey. My gratitude extends to our Peer Review Board to include: Dr. Laura Grandgenett and Dr. Gillian Silver; and our Board of Directors to include: Dr. Judy Fisher-Blando, Dr. Tom Woodruff, (and myself), and our Author Advisory Board Dr. Sheila Embry. In addition, let me offer a well deserved thank you to our production specialist, Gary Rosenberg; Refractive Thinker® logo designer, Joey Root; and our cover designer, Peri Poloni-Gabriel, Knockout Design, and companion website designer, Jacqueline Teng, maintained by AJ Shope.

Let me also extend my sincere gratitude to all participating authors within The Refractive Thinker® series who continue to believe in this project as we continue to expand our program. We appreciate their commitment to leadership and to the concept of what it means to be a refractive thinker.

Dr. Cheryl A. Lentz
Managing Editor
Las Vegas, NV
June 2011

CASE STUDY

CHAPTER 1

Learning through Case Study: The Door to Understanding

Dr. Judy Fisher-Blando and Dr. Denise L. Land

UNDERSTANDING CASE STUDY RESEARCH METHODOLOGY

Sigmund Freud (1909) was one of the first to pioneer and exploit the benefits of case study research by documenting his detailed observations about his patient Anna O. This approach, led to his subsequent development of psychoanalytical theory of personality development (Freud, 1909). In the early twenty-first century, case studies became a common research design used in social science in general, in business and management studies, in particular. The case study also has emerged as an important research design to use for both masters and doctoral-level research. According to Cooper and Schindler (2006), case study research provides understanding about the *how and why* of a situation. Case studies are commonly described as a "mostly qualitative research approach that studies one or several cases (people, organizations, processes) holistically and in their social, economic, and cultural contexts" (Eriksson & Kovalainen, 2008, p. 303). The case study design of qualitative research can provide a quality illustration and understanding of specific situations, events, perspectives, and issues.

The purpose of a case study is to gather and present evidence from multiple perspectives of a situation, event, or process (Cooper & Schindler, 2006). The design works in a number of different ways that accommodate the complexity often inherent in the business and management research process. Case studies tend to be a process for gathering a highly detailed description of perspective and situation or event information. For example, health and human service practitioners, along with general business service entities may use case study methods to understand the unique characteristics of a specific situation. "The word *unique* here is critical because the researcher is as interested in the existing conditions surrounding the person as much as the person him or herself. It is the quality of uniqueness that sets this person (and this case) apart from others" (Salkind, 2003, p. 212). Case study design allows a thorough understanding of details specific to the research focus.

According to Cooper and Schindler (2006), the research process of a case study is also "known as a *case history* that provides a case analysis or case write-up of a specific event, organization, situation, process, or activity by combining observation of activities and artifacts, along with participant interviews" (p. 217). Review of artifacts can include review of organization media, memoranda, reports, process accounting, and meeting minutes, to name a few. The observation activities of a case study generally occur in the natural setting of the interest topic or situation, and are combined with participant interviews. The objective of case study design is to gather, analyze, and report multiple perspectives of a situation, event, organization, or process at a given point in time. "The research problem is usually a how and why problem, resulting in a descriptive or explanatory study" (Cooper & Schindler, 2006, p. 217). For example, a case study process could be used to study a business process or activities, training details and results, or event activities and processes to illustrate the full scope of the situation at a given point in time.

In business research, there are fundamental differences between case study approaches. "An intensive research design focuses on finding out as much as possible on one or a few cases and the extensive design aims at mapping common patterns and properties across cases" (Eriksson & Kovalainen, 2008, p. 118). An intrinsic case is a *case* that may be selected for study because the situation or case is unusual and has merit itself (Creswell, 2002). A good case study provides and unbiased perspective and considers alternative perspectives that involve the examination of evidence from different viewpoints, and should reach a convincing result (Eriksson & Kovalainen, 2008; Simon, 2010).

CASE STUDY AS ANDRAGOGY

Case studies are often used in textbooks and popular media to provide a portrayal of occurrences in a particular organization, and to learn of the principles and practices of others. The case study is a popular research tool because of its ability to present complex issues that might be difficult to understand into accessible, clear, personal, and basic format. As a student, or one interested in an insider view from another's perspective, the *emic* approach focuses on what happens in a culture, highlighting cultural distinctions meaningful to the members of a given society (or the native point of view). Business researchers more often use an *etic* approach, which examines the extrinsic concepts and categories meaningful to an outsider's point of view (Barley, 1996). Tom Peters and Robert Waterman (1982) published *In Search of Excellence,* which provided a case study of the contributing factors that make for good business practices and excellence the nation's most successful organizations. Similar case studies include *Good to Great: Why Some Companies Make the Leap . . . and Others Don't* by Jim Collins (2001) and *Maverick: The Success Story Behind the World's Most Unusual Workplace* by Ricardo Semler (1993). Further examples of insightfully drawn cases include examinations of Disney, Microsoft, Southwest, and Google. Additionally, many professional journals, such as *The Journal of the American Medical*

Association frequently includes descriptive case studies of medically-related scenarios to illustrate patient service and organization system situations. The Harvard Business School routinely uses case study methods to portray the successes and failures of business organizations in the *Harvard Business Review* (HBR). The HBR text is a basic tool in most business-oriented curricula. Similarly, in the social science or social service arena, case studies are used to portray the experiences of individuals, children, families, gangs, and social organizations. As an example, Jonathan Kozol has written several popular books including: *Rachel and Her Children* (1989), *Savage Inequalities* (1991), and *Amazing Grace* (1995).

Particularly in process, service, or production situations in which an understanding of how or why aspects of the situation can be improved, scholarly case study research analysis can be used to study situation perspectives and evidence. Thus, as a form of pedagogy, case study activities can provide data from which analysis and learning can improve outcomes and efficiency. For example, Reynolds and Chris (2008) explored the impact of outcomes-based assessment and planning processes using case study methods in a study of college counseling centers serving the increasing psychological needs of students. Study results showed counseling centers are expected to contribute to student academic retention and success, and recommended that counseling centers can develop results-proven services and outcomes with implementation of outcomes-based assessment and planning process strategies (Reynolds & Chris, 2008).

Depending on the purpose of one's research objectives, case study methods could be applied to action research scenarios. If the purpose of research is intended to improve process efficacy, efficiency, or outcomes, the knowledge gained from case study methods could be later applied to situation systems, and then restudied in follow-up research to determine implementation outcomes. "The process is repeated until a desired outcome is reached, but along the way much is learned about the processes and about the prescriptive actions being studied. Action researchers investigate the effects of applied solutions" (Cooper & Schindler, 2006, p. 218). Essentially this would involve a cycle of situation study, data gathering, analysis, corrective action implementation, evaluation, data gathering, analysis, corrective action implementation, and evaluation (Cooper & Schindler, 2006).

TABLE 1. *ADVANTAGES AND DISADVANTAGES OF CASE STUDY RESEARCH*

Advantages

- Unique for capture human behavior and experience, particularly from a social perspective point of view
- Limited scope of one individual, event, thing, or situation
- Allows for close examination and detailed data collection
- Encourage combination of multiple techniques, such as: interviewing, survey, observation, artifact review
- Allows in-depth subject investigation
- Research results can suggest possibilities for further study.

Disadvantages

- Limited generalizability
- In-depth information gathering and observation can be time-consuming
- Reports only one perspective or reality, and therefore, include personal bias limitations
- Subject coverage is not broad or comprehensive regarding a range of situations or subjects.
- Cause and effect, in addition to speculation results are not appropriate results of case study activities and reporting.

(Salkind, 2003)

CASE STUDY AND ETHNOGRAPHY METHODS

Ethnography is similar to case study, and has many common strategies. Generally, in an ethnographic study the researcher and participant, known as a *co-researcher*, work together in a natural setting to the co-researcher to tell the story of the co-researcher experience through an unstructured dialogue and interview (Cooper & Schindler, 2006). Ethnography is more generally known as a *holistic approach* or *holistic perspective* in which researchers study the situation, event, or group from a variety of perspectives and with a variety of participants (Cooper & Schindler, 2006). Often identified as a portrayal of culture, ethnography illustrates the dynamics of a system from a variety of perspectives with a variety of methods that include direct observation, interviews, data gathering, but does not include pre-established tools such as pre-designed surveys or interview questions (Salkind, 2003). Moyo (2009) used an ethnographic study to explore how the promotion of culturally responsive pedagogy in schools might lead to narrowing students' achievement gaps, finding teachers are aware but not implementing pedagogy, and constraints such as poverty and standardized tests affect the culture surveyed.

Ethnographic methods can be combined with case study methods to yield more specific responses. For example, Waldecker (2011) used an ethnomethodological case study strategy to guide research toward understanding cross-cultural experiences of organizational learning concerning social structure and cultural values. In the Waldecker study (2011), research activities included document review, participant and event observation, audio and video recordings, and participant interviews.

The findings revealed that six learning patterns involving a clash of cultural priorities and of culture-structure interaction impeded collective learning. As a result of these findings, the researcher concluded that (a) the two cultural groups hold the same cultural values, but prioritize them in different ways; (b) each cultural group overemphasizes its prioritized values in a way that polarizes the two value systems; (c) the interaction of cultural values and structure within each group locks it into its own system, thereby impeding learning from the other group; and (d) one group tends to impose its culture structure interaction on the other when the two groups are interacting. (Waldecker, 2011, p. vi)

As demonstrated by the Waldecker (2011) application of the ethnomethodological case study, learning was achieved concerning the relevance of cross-cultural experiences concerning social structure and cultural values in the area of organizational learning.

UNDERTAKING A MASTERS OR DOCTORAL DEGREE CASE STUDY STRATEGY

As a doctoral student and studying researcher, success comes from *standing on the shoulders* of prior research and the knowledge of the scholar community. Extensive scholarly literature review of one's interest area is necessary to develop an understanding of the foundation of scholarship and knowledge previously supported through research. In particular for students and those new to the research field, it is important to note the research activities should be comprised of the next steps beyond existing research and scholarship. One's research proposal is often founded on a documented problem, which is identified and supported by recent scholarly and professional sources, and scholarly research sources that support the need for more study and research. The findings and recommendations for further study of previous research interests is the basis for taking the next steps into one's area of research interests. Similarly, research methods are often chosen based on the successful use of similar methods in previous scholarly studies.

With a desire to understand some of the failing technology policy mechanisms of United States biofuel initiatives, the Dirks (2010) study used the framework of Ostrom Institutional Analysis and Development (IAD) in a case study approach. The purpose of the Dirks study (2010) was to understand the issues of interrelated organizations and institutions that drive United States biofuel policy. The study gathered and reviewed organization artifacts, then analyzed the artifact information using the metrics of the IAD (Dirks, 2010).

Waldecker's (2011) research provides another example of this application. With an interest in cross-cultural perspectives, Waldecker (2011) combined the methods of ethnographic and case study research to answer the question "How do social structure and cultural values dynamically interact in collective learning in the context of cross-cultural experiences?" (p. 55). To lay the foundation for combining and justifying research methods, Waldecker (2011) used scholarly support to provide a foundation that justified using an ethnographic approach as the basis of his research. This explanation of the ethnographic approach acknowledged that direct interviews are not generally used or supported within an ethnographic approach as individuals themselves were not the focus of the research (ten Have, 2003). With an interest in including interviews in the proposed scope of activities, Waldecker (2011) based inclusion of the interview tactic on the advice of Merriam (1998) and Yin (2009) as justifiable in understanding the how, and why, of cross-cultural experiences in a collective learning experience of organizations and participants.

Deciding which types and how many cases to use. Case study research often includes between 4 and 15 subjects or participants to allow for *cross case* analysis and full understanding of presented perspectives from multiple sources (Cooper & Schindler, 2006.) Doctoral research generally includes the following major objectives: (a) determine area of interest and relevant document of problem to be studied; (b) locate a research population using purposeful sampling procedures; (c) identify how many cases to study; (d) receive approval from institutional review board; (e) collect extensive data using multiple forms of data collection (observations, interviews, documents, audio-visual materials); (f) guarantee provisions for respecting site and population; and (g) analyze and report the data (Creswell, 2002). Because participants are often chosen from natural settings, participant numbers may vary some from the initial research strategies proposed. For example, in the Waldecker (2011) study, the research proposal included interviewing six participants from two organizations a total of four times each; however, upon research implementation, it was determined that the interview intensity was too high and thus threatened to intimidate participants and suppress their natural response tendencies. Consequently, the interview process was modified to include 21 people interviewed up to three times each from the two organizations.

Case study as an evidence-collection approach—interview activities. According to Cooper and Schindler (2006) interviews occur with case study participants to allow participants "to tell the story of their experience" (p. 217). The interview subjects are often used to diagram different perspectives of an experience toward illustrating an in-depth understanding of an event, activity, or situation. In a dissertation entitled *Why U.S.-based Nonprofit Organizations Have a Stake in the U.S. Standing: A Case Study in Public Diplomacy,* Zatepilina (2010) used in-person executive interviews and corporate documentation to compare and synthesize the perspectives across five organizations using a theory-building technique. The Zatepilina (2010) multiple-case study finding lays the groundwork for more detailed investigation through alternative research methods, possibly ethnography, to examine more players and system elements.

Application of interview tactics is further illustrated by the Waldecker 2011 dissertation study, which incorporated interviews with 21 people from two organizations. Participants were interviewed up to three times each. The interview process was open-ended and in-depth, using a multiple interview approach with some research participants that involved follow-up interview activities based on findings and revelations of previous interviews and analysis of other study activities, including document review and observations.

Case study as an evidence-collection approach—how to analyze and interpret. The scope of case study research can include case studies across multiple organizations or events, with the intent of later cross-analysis of case study data across the multiple separate entities or events. During analysis, a single case analysis is always performed before any cross-case analysis is conducted. The emphasis is on what differences occur, why, and with what effect. Prescriptive inferences about best practices are concluded after completing case studies on several organizations or situations and are speculative in nature." (Cooper & Schindler, 2006, p. 217)

The basis of case study research findings includes data management, reduction, analysis, and interpretation (Creswell, 2002). Throughout the process of study data collection, the data must be organized to allow effective and efficient data analysis and research efficacy. Data coding allows data to be reduced to meaningful segments of understanding into broader themes for comparison in tables and figures that can serve as the basis of qualitative data analysis (Creswell, 2002). With a desire to understand how coaching can support teacher learning, Hayes (2010) examined the coaching interactions of coaches and teachers. "The analysis of the study describes how the coaches support teacher reflection and teaching for processing strategies during guided reading lessons" (Hayes, 2010, Abstract). The data analysis activity of the Hayes (2010) study was based on previous scholarly process used in similar research and advocated for by Miles and Huberman (1994).

Analysis methods included identification of primary content topics within the transcripts of research interviews, organization of data into tables and figures, and the identification of similarities and differences among the data (Hayes, 2010).

A variety of software tools, such as NVivo and Atlas.ti have been developed to assist in the data processing activity of qualitative studies that apply methods such as case study and ethnography. These resources can be used to assist in analysis of the literature review, in addition to research data organization and analysis. Use of software packages can include assistance with information analysis, which includes: (a) importing, organizing, and comparing information and data from multiple sources; (b) discovery and linkage of connections between data components; and (c) evidential justification of findings (Gregorio, 2000). Researchers interested in using software packages should contact software venders for full details.

CONCLUDING REVIEW OF CASE STUDY BENEFITS

Case study research methodology allows for limited scope research focus on one individual, event, thing, or situation with the purpose of capturing unique perspectives of human behavior and experience from a social perspective or naturalist worldview (Cooper & Schindler, 2006; Creswell, 2002; Salkind, 2003). The methodology allows for close examination of one's interest topic and detailed data collection, which encourages combination of multiple research tactics such as: interviewing, survey, observation, and document or artifact review. Finally, case study research allows for in-depth subject investigation and analysis toward promoting possibilities of further study.

REFERENCES

Barley, S. (1996). Technicians in the workplace: Ethnographic evidence for bringing work into organisations studies. *Administrative Science Quarterly,* 41:404–441.

Collins, J. (2001). *Good to great: Why some companies make the leap . . . and others don't.* New York, NY: Harper Collins Publishers, Inc.

Cooper, D. R., & Schindler, P. S. (2006). *Business research methods.* New York, NY: McGraw Hill/Irwin.

Creswell, J. (2002). *Educational research: Planning, conducting, and evaluating quantitative and qualitative research.* Upper Saddle River, NJ: Pearson Education, Inc.

Dirks, L. C. (2010). *The past and future of biofuels a case study of the United States using the institutional analysis and development framework.* (Doctoral dissertation). Retrieved from ProQuest Dissertations and Theses database. (UMI Number: 1483379)

Eriksson, P., & Kovalainen, A. (2008). *Qualitative methods in business research.* London, England: Sage Publications.

Freud, S. (1909). *Five lectures on psycho-analysis.* New York, NY: W. W. Norton & Co., Inc.

Gregorio, S. D. (2000). *Using NVivo for your literature review.* Retrieved from http://www.sdgassociates.com/downloads/literature_review.pdf

Hayes, R. S. (2010). *The study of literacy coaching observations and interviews with elementary teachers* (Doctoral dissertation). Available from ProQuest Dissertations and Theses database. (UMI Number: 3411024)

Kozol, J. (1989). *Rachel and her children: Homeless families in America.* New York, NY: Ballantine Books.

Kozol, J. (1991). *Savage inequalities: Children in America's schools.* New York, NY: Crown Publishers.

Kozol, J. (1995). *Amazing grace: The lives of children and the conscience of a nation.* New York, NY: Crown Publishers.

Merriam, S. B. (1998). *Qualitative research and case study applications in education*

(2nd ed.). San Francisco, CA: Jossey-Bass.

Miles, M. B., & Huberman, A. M. (1994). *An expanded sourcebook qualitative data analysis.* Thousand Oaks, CA: Sage Publications.

Moyo, D. (2009). *Culturally responsive pedagogy in the early childhood classroom: ethnography.* Retrieved from ProQuest Dissertations and Theses database. (UMI Number: 3419815)

Peters, T. J., & Waterman, Jr., R. H. (1982). *In search of excellence: Lessons from America's best-run companies.* New York, NY: Warner Books edition.

Reynolds, A., & Chris, S. (2008, July/August). Improving practice through outcomes based planning and assessment: A counseling center case study. *Proquest Educational Journals,* p. 374. Retrieved from http://www.ied .edu.hk/obl/files/out.pdf

Salkind, N. J. (2003). *Exploring research.* (5th ed.). Upper Saddle River, NJ: Prentice Hall, Inc.

Semler, R. (1993). *Maverick: The success story behind the world's most unusual workplace.* New York, NY: Warner Books.

Simon, M. (2010). *Dissertation & scholarly research: A practical guide to start & complete your dissertation, thesis, or formal research project.* Dissertation Success LLC.

tenHave, P. (2003). *Understanding qualitative research and ethnomethodology.* Thousand Oaks, CA: Sage Publications.

Waldecker, G. T. (2011). *Organizational earning from cross-cultural experiences: An ethnomethodological case study examining the relative importance of social structure and cultural values during dynamic interaction.* (Doctoral dissertation). Retrieved from ProQuest Dissertations and Theses database. (UMI Number: 3428075)

Yin, R. K. (2009). *Case study research: Design and methods* (3rd ed.). Thousand Oaks, CA: Sage Publications.

Zatepilina, O. (2010). *Why U.S.-based nonprofit organizations have a skate in the U.S. standing: A case study in public diplomacy.* (Doctoral dissertation). Retrieved from ProQuest Dissertations and Theses database. (UMI Number: 3437589)

About the Author

 Southern California author Dr. Judy Fisher-Blando holds several accredited degrees: a Bachelor of Science (BS) in Business Management; a Master's of Art (MA) in Organizational Management; and a Doctorate of Management (DM) in Organizational Leadership from the University of Phoenix School of Advanced Studies. She has also obtained her Six Sigma Black Belt certificate.

Dr. Judy an adjunct professor for Walden University and University of Phoenix, teaching classes in organizational behavior and research methodologies.

She is an expert on Workplace Bullying, having written her research dissertation on *Workplace Bullying: Aggressive Behavior and Its Effect on Job Satisfaction and Productivity.* In addition, she is a Life Coach, coaching leaders on how to develop High Performance Organizations, coaching the targets of workplace bullies, and giving presentations on Fining and Measuring your Joy.

To reach Dr. Judy Fisher-Blando for information on any of these topics, and for executive coaching or coaching on workplace bullying, please e-mail drjudyblando@yahoo.com

About the Author

Dr. Denise L. Land holds several accredited degrees, including a Bachelor of Science (BS) in Gerontology and Masters of Social Work from California State University, Sacramento; and a Doctorate of Management (DM) in Organizational Leadership from the University of Phoenix School of Advanced Studies.

Dr. D., as she is known to her students, is a university professor on faculty with Walden University, where she also serves on several doctoral committees and is a faculty mentor. Faculty teaching activities include strategic planning, leadership, and research methods. In addition to her faculty work with Walden, she also has university faculty experience in the areas of human services, psychology, communications, research, management, leadership, and critical thinking.

Additional published works include her dissertation: *Identifying Strategic Leadership Practice Motivators of Nonprofit Employee Retention;* and "Socio-Technical Systems Advancement: Making Distance Learning Changes That Count" *Journal of U.S. Distance Learning Association.*

To reach Dr. Denise Land for information on any of these topics, please e-mail her: dlland@ftcnet.net

CHAPTER 2

Innovative Qualitative Multiple Case Study Methodology

Dr. Armando Salas-Amaro Jr.

A s doctoral learners prepare to write their dissertations, they may determine standard research methodologies are not be suitable for their proposed study. The researcher must then adopt best practices from qualitative and quantitative designs. The chosen research methodology will result in an innovative combination of several standardized methodologies such as research design, qualitative design, multiple case study design, appropriateness of design, research questions, population, sampling frame, data collection, primary data, secondary data, research tools, instrumentation, validity and reliability, and data analysis.

The innovative qualitative multiple case study methodology was chosen for the 2007 Salas-Amaro Study and will be used to exemplify how an examination of default prevention and management practices at Florida's 28 community colleges was conducted. This article includes the problem and the elements included in the multiple case study research and demonstrates to doctoral learners that crafting unique and unusual methodologies is possible.

PROBLEM STATEMENT

Federal regulations mandate that institutions of higher learning monitor their cohort default rates. Increasing cohort default rates will trigger unscheduled program reviews, jeopardize federal funding, and negatively affect revenues for institutions (U.S. Department of Education, 2004a). The problem is that Florida's 28 community colleges have an average cohort default rate of 9.0%, which exceeds the national cohort default rate of 5.1%. The state of Florida has an average cohort default rate of 6.1%, where the national average for community colleges is 8.1%. The 2007 Salas-Amaro Study was finalized in 2007 and the latest industry data was from federal fiscal year 2004. In the past 3 federal fiscal years, 27 out of the 28 community colleges in Florida have exceeded the three cohort default rate industry averages (U.S. Department of Education, 2006a).

This qualitative multiple-case study evaluated the default prevention and management practices of Florida's 28 community colleges by interviewing 28 financial aid directors or loan coordinators. Open-ended questions were used to discover whether community colleges, all of which have higher than average default rates, have been following the default prevention and management plans recommended by the U.S. Department of Education (2006a). The responses from the financial aid directors and loan coordinators determined whether Florida's community colleges had standardized and structured default prevention and management practices.

The results of the interviews assisted in prescribing remedies for effective default prevention and management practices at Florida community colleges. The 2007 Salas-Amaro Study focused on exploring existing practices. A quantitative design used to explain relationships among variables was not appropriate for this type of research. The study did not include testing theories involving the analysis of two variables using numerical data, another characteristic of quantitative designs. Conversely, in qualitative research, flexible emerging structures and evaluative data can be used in research to enrich an analysis (Creswell, 2004). A qualitative approach was appropriately adopted for the study.

RESEARCH DESIGN

The extent to which each of the 28 community colleges in Florida adheres to the U.S. Department of Education's (2005a) default prevention and management guidelines was examined. Structured, specific default management guidelines were recommended by the researcher. As Florida's student loan default rate significantly exceeds the national average cohort default rate, studying the national average cohort default rate for community colleges and the state of Florida cohort default rate (U.S. Department of Education, 2005) to explore the phenomenon and to identify potential causes seemed critical. A qualitative design was appropriate to this central phenomenon.

Financial aid directors or loan coordinators at each of Florida's 28 community colleges were interviewed. A series of open-ended interview questions was used to determine whether existing default prevention and management practices at the community colleges aligned with the U.S. Department of Education's (2005a) default prevention recommendations. Combining the results from the interviews with current literature using triangulation increased the confidence in the data's reliability (Creswell, 2002). After the results from the interviews were collected and analyzed, the 2007 Salas-Amaro Study proposed a structured default prevention and management plan.

The purposeful sampling method was used to recruit participants. Creswell (2004) stated researchers use purposeful sampling to select individuals and sites, such as college campuses, to learn about a central phenomenon. In the case of this qualitative multiple-case study, 28 financial aid directors or loan coordinators were interviewed. These individuals are responsible for implementing financial aid policies and procedures at their institutions. If the financial aid directors were not available, then the loan coordinators were interviewed in their place.

QUALITATIVE DESIGN

A qualitative research case study presents a research problem to better examine a central phenomenon. The extent to which each of the 28 community colleges adhered to the U.S. Department of Education's (2005a) default management guidelines was determined, and recommendations for the implementation of structured, specific default management guidelines were made.

MULTIPLE-CASE STUDY DESIGN

In a variety of disciplines, researchers have used the multiple-case study method (Creswell, 2004) as a mechanism for examining complex issues. Yin (1984) explained case study research is "an empirical inquiry that investigates a contemporary phenomenon within its real-life context, when the boundaries between phenomenon and context are not clearly evident and in which multiple sources of evidence is used" (p. 23). Some researchers have dismissed case study research because the scenario and evidence involved may not be applicable in all situations; but others have successfully used the method and have carefully planned studies of real-life situations, problems, and issues (Yin, 1984). This research adopted techniques from Simon (2006), who suggested six techniques for planning and organizing research successfully: (a) determining and defining research questions; (b) determining data gathering and analyzing techniques; (c) preparing to collect the data; (d) collecting data in the field; (e) evaluating and analyzing data; and (f) preparing the report.

The steps taken in the case study method included (a) defining the research questions; (b) gathering data through phone interviews with financial aid administrators; (c) tallying the results from the phone interviews in a spreadsheet; (d) analyzing the data by classifying the community colleges in columns and the interview questions with their answers in rows; (e) finding themes and commonalities; and (f) processing the analysis. This process enabled a thorough examination of the data and the ability to make determinations regarding the current standard practices.

APPROPRIATENESS OF DESIGN

As the study focused on exploring existing practices, a qualitative approach was the best methodological choice. According to Patton (2002), qualitative research explores non-numerical data patterns or themes to answer the research questions and close knowledge gaps. Maxwell (2005).explained that a phenomenon explored in its institutional context and from the participants' viewpoint is largely lost when the textual data are quantified. Maxwell (2005) observed that qualitative approaches have advantages of flexibility, in-depth analysis, and observation of various aspects of a situation. Qualitative research is used to examine factors such as human behavior in the social, cultural, and political context (Salkind, 2003).

Qualitative methods are helpful when one wishes to understand and concentrate on how something happens. Conversely, quantitative designs are more appropriate to determine and measure outcomes. Qualitative approaches focus on the participants' experiences, their knowledge base, and their perceptions (Patton, 2002).

The 2007 Salas-Amaro Study explored the current default prevention and management practices in place at all community colleges in Florida to determine why their cohort default rates exceeded the national average in the fiscal years 2002, 2003, and 2004. The qualitative multiple-case study was guided by three research questions:

1. What default prevention and management practices are currently in place at Florida's 28 community colleges?

2. How closely do community colleges' current default prevention

and management activities align with the U.S. Department of Education's guidelines?

3. What guidelines are financial aid administrators implementing to reduce their community college's cohort default rate?

The research questions were used to obtain data regarding how closely Florida's community colleges' default prevention and management practices aligned with the recommended guidelines from the U.S. Department of Education (2005a). This study was crucial to discover whether the financial aid administrators were implementing default prevention and management methods and formulating any type of standardized default prevention practices.

POPULATION

The population of interest for the study was comprised 28 financial aid administrators, such as financial aid directors and loan coordinators, from Florida's community college system. The community colleges are located within the six regions of the state. The six regions are (a) north Florida known as the Panhandle, (b) the Crown, (c) east central Florida, (d) west central Florida, (e) southeast Florida, and (f) south Florida. These regions are located between Pensacola and Key West (Florida Department of Education, 2006).

Community college financial aid directors usually have a minimum of 5 years of experience in student financial assistance, and some community colleges may require that they hold a master's degree. Loan coordinators or default managers may be required to have a minimum of 2 years' financial aid experience and hold a bachelor's degree (citation). These individuals usually begin working in financial aid after obtaining a bachelor's degree. Some financial aid administrators have experience in other areas of higher education.

Community college financial aid directors may already be members of financial aid organizations such as the Florida Association of Student Financial Aid Administrators, the Southern Association of Financial Aid Administrators, and the National Association of Student Financial Aid Administrators. These organizations focus on bringing financial aid administrators together, providing training, and creating a communication network among the financial aid community.

The telephone interviews with the financial aid directors and loan coordinators focused on discovering the default prevention and management practices currently in place at each community college. Dr. Salas-Amaro gained specific insight into how financial aid administrators coordinated the student loan process and generated more effective default prevention practices. The interviews determined those factors which differentiated community colleges in the Florida community college system that had lower default rates from those that with higher default rates. As an aggregate, all the community colleges in Florida are experiencing higher than the national average (Florida Department of Education, 2006).

SAMPLING FRAME

Purposeful sampling is a judgmental form of sampling that can be used to examine data in depth. Specifically, this approach was used in the Salas-Amaro 2007 Study to select individuals to learn or understand a central phenomenon (Creswell, 2004). Individuals are information rich (Patton, 2002). The financial aid directors and loan coordinators from Florida's 28 community colleges were knowledgeable in financial aid procedures and policies, and they were responsible for implementing the related policies. After this timeframe, institutions already received a draft of their cohort default rate and it is adequate timing to make a determination of whether their current default prevention and management practices were all inclusive and comprehensive. As institutions should have already reviewed cohort default data for the fiscal year 2005 prior to the study, the interviews provided an opportunity to obtain recent information about their current processes.

DATA COLLECTION

This qualitative multiple-case study examined the default prevention and management practices of Florida's 28 community colleges by conducting structured telephone interviews with pre-qualified participants. As the community colleges were geographically dispersed throughout Florida, most financial aid directors or loan coordinators were unable to meet in one central location. Creswell (2004) explained that a telephone interview is the process of gathering data using the telephone with an adaptor plug and tape recorder for a clearly-recorded interview. A small number of general questions were asked in the study, and they followed the technique of extending a combination of purposeful broad, general, and specific questions to participants. This approach enabled participants to share open views that were unconstrained by researcher's perspectives (Creswell, 2004).

Primary Data

It was important to investigate why some community colleges had lower default rates than others. Collecting factual information assisted in determining the default prevention and management practices at Florida's 28 community colleges. Yin (2003) recommended that the collection of comprehensive and systematic data allows the researcher to reference, sort, and carefully analyze the data so that patterns of inquiry can be uncovered. The categorization and referencing of data thereby make information readily available. This methodology contributed to the delivery of exemplary case studies. The interview questions were developed to collect information on default prevention and management procedures. The participants were interviewed to discover each individual institution's default prevention and management practices, characteristics of students admitted, student's income level, retention rate, graduation rate, and student loan volume. The research revealed whether community colleges should be more proactive in formulating default prevention and management plans to curb student loan defaults.

Secondary Data

Default rate materials and default rates for Florida's 28 community colleges were available from the U.S. Department of Education's (2006a) Information for Financial Aid Professionals web site. Factual evidence, such as trends and statistics, was gathered from the Florida Board of Education, Division of Community Colleges, and the American Association of Community Colleges. This process was performed to enable triangulation of the results. These resources assisted in deriving more meaning from the responses of the financial aid directors or loan coordinators (Leedy & Ormrod, 2001). The findings from the interviews and the review of current practices were combined and compared to increase confidence in the data's reliability (Creswell, 2002).

RESEARCH TOOLS

In the data collection and data analysis processes, qualitative case studies require the use of various research tools. The study included Internet sources utilized in the literature review and for secondary data. Primary data were obtained with the telephone and tape recorder.

Internet. Federal and State of Florida government web sites, such as Information for Financial Aid Professionals, Florida Board of Education, Division of Community Colleges, and the American Association of Community Colleges, were used to retrieve Florida's community colleges' characteristics. These secondary data supported the responses to the interview questions and validated the findings.

Telephone and tape recorder. Use of a tape recorder enabled the researcher to (a) listen to the recording and find what might have been missed in the written notes, (b) capture insights that were not initially perceived, and (c) directly focus on the participant being interviewed (Creswell, 2004). An adaptor was used for the telephone and recorder to obtain a clear interview.

Spreadsheet. The qualitative data were examined in a spreadsheet. The community colleges were listed in columns, and the research questions, along with their answers, were listed in rows. This method of displaying the data facilitated the analysis of data and put potential commonalities among the institutions' practices in evidence.

INSTRUMENTATION

In a qualitative case study, the primary instrument of data collection is the researcher (Simon, 2006). In the study, information was obtained from the telephone interviews to examine whether the current default prevention and management practices aligned with the U.S. Department of Education's (2005a) recommended guidelines. Maxwell (2005) explained that qualitative researchers test the validity of the information throughout the collection and analytical processes, thereby ensuring the data are as free of bias as possible.

PILOT STUDY

A pilot study uses a sub-set of the sample not to be tested in a final study. In qualitative and quantitative designs, a pilot study can test sampling methods, design, data collection methods, instrument reliability and validity, and data analysis (Sproull, 2004). The pilot study is a crucial element of a good study design, and the pilot is a small-scale version of a larger study. In this qualitative multiple-case study, the pilot study contributed validity to the interview questions that were used in the final study.

The pilot study was conducted with five participants: Florida Department of Education employees, student loan lender representatives, and selected college employees who would not have the same information as the selected participants for the study. The pilot study was used to diagnose any problems with interview questions before implementation of the final study.

The participants for the pilot study were a sub-set of the population used in the final study. Participants were given the informed consent form, and asked to return it via e-mail or fax to the researcher. If this letter was e-mailed, signatures were to be preceded by /s/ to indicate an electronic signature. By signing the informed consent form, the participant indicated he or she was 18 years or older, agreed to participate in the study, understood the potential risks, and acknowledged she or he could withdraw at any time by refusing to answer any questions. The informed consent forms were kept securely in a locked drawer cabinet for 3 years, and then shredded and destroyed. Based on the results from the pilot study, questions were changed to ensure face validity. The outcomes of a pilot study will allow doctoral learners to revise research questions and ensure that the questions are appropriate, free of bias, and open-ended. The accuracy and effectiveness of the questions will avoid interruptions throughout the study and interview phase.

VALIDITY AND RELIABILITY

Creswell (2004) explained that with qualitative research, one explores patterns or themes to answer research questions or close knowledge gaps while avoiding biases and finding reliable data. Consistency found in the data increased the reliability of the research study (Yin, 2003). After discerning the themes found in the data, it was possible to determine whether there was a pattern in the practices of financial aid directors or loan coordinators who were not adhering to the recommended default prevention guidelines by the U.S. Department of Education.

Member validation is a technique used for the respondents to provide feedback, but qualitative researchers are more likely to address validity throughout the data collection and analysis processes (Maxwell, 2005). Qualitative researchers review cases to ensure validity by seeking patterns and common themes (Maxwell, 2005). The research questions were formulated to focus on community colleges' compliance with federal guidelines that recommend effective default prevention and management practices. In the Salas-Amaro 2007 Study, the pilot study was used to diagnose any problems with interview questions and to establish face validity before implementing the final study

DATA ANALYSIS

Creswell (2004) detailed five steps qualitative researchers use to analyze and interpret data: (a) organizing the data to be analyzed; (b) exploring the data; (c) describing and developing themes from the data; (d) reporting the findings; and (e) validating the credibility and accuracy of the findings. In the Salas-Amaro 2007 Study, the data were manually collected from the telephone interviews and organized in a spreadsheet. The participants' answers to each interview question were then analyzed by grouping all of the answers from each participant and analyzing individual responses to the questions. The following themes were discovered: a) Community colleges did not have standardized default prevention practices in place; b) Financial aid directors and loan coordinators only followed the minimum required elements of entrance and exit counseling; and c) they did not perform additional default prevention methods to ensure successful student loan repayment. The data collected were analyzed several times to ensure a full understanding of the data before dividing them in sections according to theme (Agar, 1980).

The data collected from the telephone interviews were manually analyzed because the database had fewer than 500 pages (Creswell, 2004). The data were organized in various categories, and themes were developed based on the different or similar policies and procedures the community colleges had in place for default prevention and management practices. The processed data were reported in a word processing document to reveal the findings of the analysis in chapter 4 of the dissertation. The data were organized in a narrative discussion. Creswell (2004) stated that the qualitative study could be written in a narrative form to summarize and analyze findings. The narrative has no set form and can vary from one study to another.

The final step of the data analysis was the interpretation of the findings. Maxwell (2005) recommended that clear meaning be extracted from the findings. In the Salas-Amaro 2007 study, meaning was found in the responses to interview questions by the participating financial aid directors or loan coordinators. When interpreting the data, the findings, along with information from the literature review, were used to relate the outcome of this research to past studies. The analysis was a manual process, and each financial aid director and loan coordinator had a file assigned to her or him. The answers to each interview question from each financial aid director or loan coordinator was analyzed by grouping all of the answers from each participant and analyzing individual responses to the questions.

CONCLUSION

The innovative qualitative multiple case study presented in the Salas-Amaro 2007 Study included a discussion of the qualitative design chosen to successfully complete a study on the default prevention and management practices in Florida's 28 community colleges. A purposeful sampling method was used, and the data obtained from telephone interviews were analyzed. The research questions, population, sampling frame, participant consent, confidentiality, geographic location, design appropriateness, reliability, and validity were discussed. The innovative approach offers doctoral learners insight into a suitable alternative research method. As at the time of the study there had not been any other research studies conducted on default prevention and management practices at Florida community college, an innovative multiple case study methodology proved both appropriate and valuable.

REFERENCES

Agar, M. H. (1980). *The professional stranger: An informal introduction to ethnography.* San Diego, CA: Academic Press.

Creswell, J. W. (2004). *Education research: Planning, conducting and evaluating quantitative and qualitative research* (2nd ed.). Columbus, OH: Merrill Prentice Hall.

Florida Department of Education. (2006). Retrieved from http://www .fldoe.org

Leedy, P. D., & Ormrod, J. E. (2001). *Practical research: Planning and design* (7th ed.). Upper Saddle River, NJ: Merrill Prentice Hall.

Maxwell, J. (2005). *Qualitative research design: An interactive approach* (2nd ed.). Thousand Oaks, CA: Sage.

Patton, M. Q. (2002). *Qualitative research and evaluation methods* (3rd ed.). Thousand Oaks, CA: Sage.

Salkind, N. J. (2003). *Exploring research* (5th ed.). Upper Saddle River, NJ: Prentice Hall.

Sproull, N. D. (2004). *Handbook of research methods: A guide for practitioners and students in the social sciences* (3rd ed.). Lanham, MD: The Scarecrow Press.

U.S. Department of Education. (2004a). *Student financial aid handbook.* Washington, DC: U.S. Government Printing Office.

United States Department of Education. (2005a). *Code of Federal Regulations (CFR) 668.14(b) (15) stated in Dear Colleague Letter DCL: GEN 05–14, 2005.* Retrieved from http://www.ifap.ed.gov/dpcletters/GEN0514 .html

U.S. Department of Education. (2006a). *Dear colleague letter GEN 06-02.* Retrieved from http://www.ifap.ed.gov/dpcletters/attachments/GEN-06-02A.pdf

APPENDIX A					
	FY 2002			**FY 2003**	
Public	1,681	5.1%	66,297	1,295,318	1,663	4.3%
Less than 2 yrs	165	6.7%	396	5,851	159	5.8%
2–3 yrs	908	8.5%	25,695	299,379	895	7.6%
4yrs(+)	608	4.0%	40,206	990,088	609	3.3%
Private	1,837	3.2%	22,019	669,099	1,812	2.8%
Less than 2 yrs	65	9.7%	289	2,954	55	7.9%
2–3 yrs	248	6.1%	1,348	21,959	247	6.3%
4yrs(+)	1,524	3.1%	20,382	644,186	1,510	2.6%
Proprietary	2,000	8.7%	37,269	423,631	1,950	7.3%
Less than 2 yrs	1,131	10.1%	11,092	108,748	1,054	7.9%
2–3 yrs	681	9.2%	14,801	160,432	688	8.0%
4 yrs(+)	188	7.3%	11,376	154,451	208	6.4%
Foreign	436	2.0%	111	5,434	411	1.8%
Unclassified	1	0.0%	0	294	1	0.0%
TOTAL	5,955	5.2%	125,696	2,393,776	5,837	4.5%

*Note: These rates are accurate only as of September 11, 2006. The table reflects all borrowers who entered repayment during the given fiscal year as reported to the National Student Loan Database System (NSLDS). Some of these borrowers attended schools that are no longer eligible for Title IV program participation. The information provided in the downloadable or searchable reports is limited to schools that, at the time of the most recent calculation, were eligible for participation in the Title IV programs.

FY 2003		FY 2004			
59,460	1,356,086	1,647	4.7%	70,864	1,488,978
359	6,182	153	5.7%	390	6,808
25,259	328,730	889	8.1%	31,476	386,474
33,842	1,021,174	605	3.5%	38,998	1,095,696
19,523	695,576	1,790	3.0%	22,434	741,372
265	3,326	55	9.0%	353	3,881
1,477	23,160	233	7.4%	1,526	20,539
17,781	669,090	1,502	2.8%	20,555	716,952
36,477	493,895	1,963	8.6%	50,729	588,432
9,302	117,166	1,046	8.9%	11,755	130,810
14,469	179,553	697	9.9%	20,346	205,000
12,706	197,176	220	7.3%	18,628	252,622
108	5,844	434	1.5%	100	6,662
0	31	2	5.5%	1	18
115,568	2,551,432	5,836	5.1%	144,128	2,825,462

About the Author

 Dr. Armando Salas-Amaro has been in higher education for over 16 years. Currently, he is the Department Chair of the Leadership Concentration in the MBA Program at Keiser University and remains an active associate faculty member for University of Phoenix School of Business. Prior to joining Keiser University, Dr. Armando was an Education Policy Analyst for the Florida Department of Education, Office of Student Financial Assistance (OSFA). Dr. Armando has also contributed to ECPI College of Technology and Herzing University, and worked as a financial aid administrator for Miami-Dade College.

Dr. Armando serves on the following committees: Florida Association of Postsecondary Schools and Colleges (FAPSC) Continuing Education Committee, formerly on Mapping-Your-Future where he earned an excellence award in 2009, and the National Association of Tax Professionals (NATP) along with the Florida Chapter of NATP. During Dr. Armando's years of service to the Florida Department of Education, he was actively involved in the Florida Association of Student Financial Aid Administrators (FASFAA) as a presenter/trainer, the National Association of Student Financial Aid Administrator (NASFAA), and the Southern Association of Student Financial Aid Administrators (SASFAA).

Dr. Armando's doctoral dissertation was on default prevention and management practices at Florida Community Colleges. Dr. Armando has also been the guest speaker in *CollegeWeek Live* and in *"Este es El Momento"* with Univision.

To reach Dr. Armando for information on any of these topics, please e-mail armandoii@hotmail.com

ETHNOGRAPHY

CHAPTER 3

Improving Business Performance Through Ethnographic Research

Dr. Ramon L. Benedetto

Katzenbach and Harshak (2011) noted culture invariably trumps strategy when a company is at risk because a company's identity is "grounded in the way people think and behave" (p. 36). Executing strategy invariably requires change, which can create resistance if not handled effectively. Many leaders are quick to blame company culture, i.e., the deeply embedded beliefs and practices that distinguish a company, as the root of change resistance rather than embracing the culture as a tool for advancing change, increasing organizational effectiveness, and achieving outcomes (Katzenbach & Harshak, 2011).

Company culture includes organizational values that help to guide employee behaviors within organizations (Hitt, 1990). These values, which originate within each employee, define employee behaviors by which the corporation or business performs and rewards or sanctions outcomes (Argandoña, 2003). The values that underpin organizational culture are foundational guides of intrinsic importance to people within an organization (Chun, 2005; Collins & Porras, 1994). Despite the reluctance of some leaders to acknowledge the importance of values in driving behaviors and results, values directly influence views and behaviors, which then have a direct impact on relations within a company as well as with external parties (Meglino & Ravlin, 1998).

Values in action represent the character of individuals, and organizational values collectively practiced represent the character of an organization (Benedetto, 2010). Organizational culture takes some attributes from the experiences and backgrounds of the employees, i.e., their characters as well as their knowledge (Katzenbach & Harshak, 2011). Leaders who use a value-based approach directly influence the internal ethical climate of a company, creating a positive culture through which employees strengthen relationships and achieve positive results (Grojean, Resick, Dickson, & Smith, 2004).

In contrast, ethical problems within organizations have emerged in recent scandals because of conflicts between social norms within organizations and individual values (Maheshwari & Ganesh, 2006). If leaders expect ethical decision-making throughout an organization, then training programs must define and teach organizational values and ethics and the culture must reinforce ethical choices (Bowen, 2004). Since business ethics are rules of conduct, ethics share a position with values as a foundational part of organizational culture (Schein, 2004).

Understanding how values and ethics operate within an organization resides with ethnographic research, which is the study of culture and the various frames of meaning that exist within a specific culture (Agar, 1986). Atkinson, Coffey, Delamont, Lofland, and Lofland (2007) noted that "first-hand exploration of research settings" (p. 5) is the critical difference between ethnographic research and other methods and this sense of "social exploration . . . gives ethnography its abiding and continuing character" (p. 5). This research study reflected a key principle of ethnography: ethnographers must draw on "a very diverse repertoire of research techniques" (Atkinson et al., 2007, p. 5), which include structural and textual analysis of narratives, interviews, and company documents as well as the collection and interpretation of visual images. This chapter strives to show the value of this methodology and these techniques in revealing cultural attributes that contribute to business success.

THE PROBLEM COMPANY LEADERS FACE AND STUDY OVERVIEW

Key (1999) noted the conceptual foundation of organizational culture resides in anthropology because culture defines the patterns of "thinking, feeling, and reacting" [within a society and represents the] "beliefs, norms, and practices" (p. 218) that individuals share within a group. Within organizations, employees define the ways any organization "looks, feels, and behaves" (Schneider, 1987, p. 437) to outsiders; they also help define the values, beliefs, and assumptions through which a company operates. Company culture is more than the artifacts that represent a company, such as a logo, building, legends, heroes, or language. According to Schein (as cited in Benedetto, 2009), culture includes organizational philosophy and internal practices, the values that underpin behaviors, and the actions employees demonstrate habitually (p. 82).

Business leaders who are inattentive to their company cultures and the values and motives of employees with respect to ethical behavior must invariably deal with dysfunctional interactions and less than acceptable results (Dickson, Smith, Grojean, & Ehrhart, 2001). Oft times, these leaders blame company culture rather than their own behaviors for these situations and fail to acknowledge their own roles in creating, shaping, or nurturing of that culture (Katzenbach & Harshak, 2011). Effective leaders are those who strive to understand what works within a culture, capitalize on the strengths of that culture, and create opportunities for behaviors to become contagious carriers of new and better ways for doing business (Katzenbach & Harshak, 2011). This study showed how the leaders within a specific company prove this point.

THE PURPOSE AND FOUNDATION OF ETHNOGRAPHIC RESEARCH

The subject of this study was a very successful catering company in northern Illinois that began as a hot dog stand where "the values of quality, quantity, and service [were] the cornerstones to company success" (Benedetto, 2009, p. 205). These values created the demand for catering services, which eventually required a significant company expansion in staff and infrastructure and complete divestiture of the restaurant business. Unlike some expansions that create a whole new company culture, the subject company stayed true to its core values, driving more business and deepening cultural roots in the process. This ethnography examined and explored how employees at all company levels lived the culture within various company domains, from frontline, customer-centric delivery and service to behind-the-scene coordination of actions that consistently led to exceptional customer satisfaction and business growth.

Ethnographic studies involve the lived experiences of people within a culture, thus ethnographers who study these cultures must engage several disciplines, such as anthropology, psychology, and sociology (Schwartzman, 1993). Within the context of business administration and management, ethnographic studies reveal critical information about the formal and informal organizations that exist within business, requiring business ethnographers to also have a deep knowledge and appreciation for leadership and management disciplines (Schwartzman, 1993). Ethnographies require narratives and story-telling by people within the study as well as analysis of the language and communications within a culture (Atkinson et al., 2007). The dialogue and communication within personal interactions such as company meetings represent cultural language through which leaders relay messages across organizational levels and boundaries (Schwartzman, 1993). Employees also create personal meanings about an organization through the experiences they connect to stories told by leaders in meetings, on the shop floor, and within company communications such as newsletters and electronic mail (Benedetto, 2009).

Cultural research requires extensive study because the underlying nuances and elements of a culture are usually revealed over time rather than simultaneously. Deeply held beliefs and operating assumptions of employees become evident through their actions, but these actions must be observed over time to assess consistency. Any description of organizational culture must emerge through intimate study and physical immersion of the researcher into various settings in which employees operate (Van Maanen, 1982).

To describe a business culture effectively, researchers must gain as much information as possible from multiple perspectives within and outside a company. Business culture cannot be separated from the outside world of customers, suppliers, vendors, visitors, board members, or other external parties with whom company employees interact. The trust and caring employees show toward external parties consistently become part of the company's character, i.e., the strengths for which the company is known (Benedetto, 2010).

Ethnographic design is the preferred research platform for understanding organizational culture because "ethnography seeks a detailed and comprehensive description of a people" (Angrosino, 2007, p. xv) through fieldwork that involves direct observation within a community for an extended period (Benedetto, 2009). Understanding a company's culture requires intense, iterative study over an extended period that may span several months or longer. Unlike quantitative research that seeks to prove hypotheses, research questions guide ethnographic research, which evolves as new information becomes known through observations, narrative inquiries and interviews, and archival research, all of which add to the complexity and richness of ethnographic study.

COMPARISON OF OTHER QUALITATIVE METHODS TO ETHNOGRAPHIC RESEARCH

Ethnographic research is not a widely practiced form of qualitative research. However, its contribution to the study and understanding of organizational culture is profound. The following sections provide a brief comparative analysis of various qualitative research methods from which a better understanding of ethnographic research should emerge.

Grounded Theory

Grounded theory seeks to unravel elements of experience from which a theory emerges about the "nature and meaning of an experience for a particular group of people in a particular setting" (Moustakas, 1994. p. 4). Two tenets of grounded theory are (a) the theory and data emerge from interviews instead of observations related to individual practices, and (b) theory must "grow out of data and be grounded in that data" (Addison, 1989, p. 41). A primary characteristic of grounded theory design is the "constant comparison of data with emerging categories and theoretical sampling of different groups" [through which] "the similarities and differences of information" (Creswell, 2003, p. 14) are maximized.

Grounded theory and ethnographies are related because each focuses on consciousness and experience as research essentials, but data about specific cultures is commonly missing, which would void grounded theory as a viable research option for studying culture (Moustakas, 1994). Ethnography is often confused with grounded theory because some ethnographic studies must espouse some theory (Stewart, 1998). Whereas grounded theory concentrates on generating a theory from data obtained through interviews, interviews alone cannot explain a culture when intense observation of individual practices or behaviors is necessary (Addison, 1989).

Narrative Inquiry and Phenomenology

Narrative inquiry requires a deep and rich study of the lives of one or more individuals, from which the views of those studied combine with those of the researcher through a collaborative narrative

(Clandinin & Connelly, 2000). Clandinin and Connelly (2000) described the focus of narrative inquiry as "the lived experience of one or more individuals rather than an entire community or culture" (as cited in Benedetto, 2009, p. 11). In contrast to narrative inquiry, phenomenology looks at a specific phenomenon from the perspectives of many study participants rather than merely a few (Creswell, 2003). The emphasis of phenomenology on a specific phenomenon as viewed by several people stands in stark contrast to the pervasive, systemic aspects of organizational culture (Creswell, 2003).

Unlike other studies where researchers are anxious to get into an organization to investigate a specific phenomenon, event, or anomaly, ethnography involves *everything* about an organization, including the manner in which first encounters unfold as part of ethnographic observation (Schwartzman, 1993). Ethnography can be easily confused with a naturalistic research paradigm where multiple realities co-exist, the parties within an organization operate interdependently and independently, inquiry is value bound, and the research must occur in the natural setting of the organizational context (Lincoln & Guba, 1985). The key differentiators between ethnography and other naturalistic research are the depth and breadth of research associated with understanding an entire culture. Ethnography is analogous to a tapestry whereas narrative inquiry and phenomenology are similar to patchwork quilts.

Case Study

According to Lincoln and Guba (1985), case studies have no single purpose in mind nor does a simple taxonomy exist for classifying the various uses of case studies. Case studies vary by purpose, analytic level, audience, and other factors, and usually attempt to address a single problem (Lincoln & Guba, 1985) Case study and ethnographic approaches both involve studies over a sustained period, but the critical difference between the two options is case studies explore a specific program, event, activity, or process involving one or more individuals (Creswell, 2003). In contrast to ethnographies, case studies do not study an entire culture where numerous programs and events, multiple processes, and many individuals are involved or engaged. LeCompte and Schensul (1999b) argued that although case studies can be effective, naturalistic inquiries within the bounds of a specific activity and time period, these studies are ineffective and inadequate for understanding the many facets of organizational culture that emerge over time (as cited in Benedetto, 2009).

Ethnography

Angrosino (2007) defined ethnography as "the art and science of describing a human group-its institutions, interpersonal behaviors, material productions, and beliefs" (p. 14). Benedetto (2009) asserted, "Organizational ethnographers seek to understand the cultural knowledge, behavior, language, institutions, interpersonal behaviors, and beliefs that employees have in common and use to shape and interpret experiences" (p. 132), using the works of Angrosino (2007), Schwartzman (1993), and Spradley (1980) as a foundation. According to Agar (as cited in Benedetto, 2009), "Ethnography includes understanding different meanings of words and expressions that depend on traditions, history, and the unique views of each participant" (p. 132). These meanings can only emerge during long periods of field study when patterns of communication become evident.

Ethnography does not conform to the traditional methods of qualitative research because various and often complex arrays of information call for compilation and transformation into written accounts that more closely estimate anthropological studies (Atkinson, 1992). Ethnographic approach helps tell a deep and rich story about culture within a subject company. Despite efforts to create a well-defined and detailed research plan before beginning any ethnography, the specific framework of the study will morph as the ethnography evolves and the cultural description of the company emerges from the data.

Ethnographic research includes three key components: (a) archival research into company documents and other artifacts of organizational culture; (b) narrative inquiry that includes interviews with people within and outside the culture; and (c) observations of behaviors and performance through all facets of the company (Angrosino, 2007). Long periods of field research are the most potent tactic ethnographers have for ensuring the accuracy of research (Stewart, 1998). Unlike other forms of research where teams can be used to collect, analyze, and interpret data, ethnography depends heavily on the work of a single, lone ethnographer who serves as planner, coordinator, collection point, and repository, almost simultaneously.

The exact research period depends on several factors, not the least important being the objectives and research questions that should drive the design and execution of the study. Ethnographic research is unique because the researcher must be careful to ignore personal biases and serve as a *tabula rasa* while conducting research. The researcher also faces the threat of becoming part of the environment rather than standing distinct and apart; 'going native' is a very real threat that can skew and prejudice study results. Ethnographic research is not for the faint of heart because long, isolated periods of research are part and parcel to the methodology, which demands intense personal discipline by the researcher.

ETHNOGRAPHIC METHODOLOGY WITHIN A BUSINESS CULTURE

Three overarching research questions drove the design for the 2009

Benedetto Study. The questions sought to (a) uncover how leaders built and integrated a culture of character; (b) define the unique characteristics and the stages of development of this type culture; and (c) describe how the culture affected external customers. The theoretical framework that evolved from the research questions required an extensive literature review in six areas: (a) business ethics and ethical business practices, (b) management and leadership practices, (c) virtue theory, (d) values, (e) culture, and (f) character. The depth of analysis mirrored the perspective that ethnographies are deep studies that require understanding and connecting multiple disciplines in practice (Benedetto, 2009).

Because ethnographic study requires interactions with human subjects, protecting the identity, privacy, and confidentiality of personal data was critical for validation and study success (Cone & Foster, 1999). The design of the reported study included nearly 350 hours of direct observations of employees throughout all phases of company performance. Observations reflected the communication, language, and relations between employees as internal customers within a company as well as relations between employees and selected external customers who contributed to the financial success of the company. Firsthand observation was critical for gaining data to understand the organizational setting and culture (Patton, 1990).

Narrative inquiry included 60 first and second-level interviews with three founders, seven leaders, twelve employees, and five advisers who disclosed individual views on company culture. Four client and two key supplier interviews revealed how clients, customers, and suppliers viewed company culture based on observations of employee behaviors. Two panels of randomly selected employees were used to validate the reliability of findings that emerged from interviews and observations.

Archival research and exploration included examination of company documents that described organizational history and culture such as records of meetings, internal company communications such as electronic mail, comments from current and past customers, and other cultural artifacts. This company used information technology (IT) extensively to manage daily production, customer feedback, and future work projections. A notable practice was the customer relationship management (CRM) component of the IT system, where team leaders entered comments from customers within hours of completing an assignment so everyone in the company had virtually immediate access to customer comments for follow-up actions, if necessary.

Archival research revealed feedback from past customers through company documentation. The research created a detailed narrative of the company from which a better understanding of character-based culture emerged, including how company employees translated emotions, beliefs, values, and ethos into action and engagement. Jones (2006) aptly described this translation as organizational energy.

MAJOR ASPECTS OF DATA COLLECTION

Informed Consent

Informed consent is common to all human subject research but required additional considerations within the context of this ethnographic study. The selected company employed a large number of part-time employees during the summer season in addition to 50 full-time staff. These workforce variances required several layers of informed consent that other researchers should consider when designing ethnographic studies.

Permanent and part-time employees. Permanent employees used English and Spanish as primary languages, thus Informed Consents were designed and translated to minimize potential misunderstanding because of language differences. A company employee served as an in-house translator and assisted during some interviews, which required having a confidentiality statement on record for the translator. The company also employed a large number of part-time employees when this study occurred. To avoid complications with human subject research and minor children, interviews and observations were limited to employees 18 years of age and older. The first five returning college students completed their Informed Consent forms within 24 hours of reporting for work and participated in short interviews shortly thereafter from which a short survey was developed and administered to other part-time workers participating in crew leader training. Since all crew leaders used English as their primary language, interpretation and translation services were not necessary for this cohort.

External parties. Although the study focused on the employees within a company as a community and culture, the culture extended beyond the employees. These external elements engaged an additional level of complexity that had to be addressed since they were affected by the company's culture. Gaining a comprehensive view of the company required adding interviews with customers, suppliers, and advisers. The defined "community" for the company extended to customers to whom company employees traveled to deliver goods and services and to suppliers and advisers on whom company leaders depended for their success. Although the original research design anticipated customer interviews, supplier and advisor interviews were post-start additions.

Instrumentation

Ethnographic study examines practical activities, circumstances, and sociological reasoning as phenomena in their own ways (Coulon, 1995). Ethnography also discerns the predictability and patterns of behaviors that emerge through daily routines of the people and culture rather than describing all possible interactions (Angrosino, 2007). Interview protocols for each employee category constituted the primary data collection instruments before the study began, but a self-designed survey of part-time summer workers and a validation survey were added as these needs arose. Separate interview protocols were also designed for company founders, randomly selected customers, advisers, and suppliers. Unlike quantitative research that seeks to prove a specific hypothesis, qualitative interviews are flexible and content-sensitive such that the interview is an iterative process of hypothesis testing that begins with direct questions, which subsequently evolve to counter, leading, and probing questions (Kvale, 2007). The interviews provided a collective perspective on the culture as a whole, from which general findings emerged in response to the research questions.

Primary Data Collection Tools

The study used several data collection tools described by Patton (1990), Angrosino (2007), and LeCompte and Schensul (1999b). According to Angrosino (2007), ethnographers must be skillful in archival research, observation, and interviewing.

Archival research. Exploring the history, language, and context within which employees worked and how the company evolved since its founding was a precursor to field observations and interviews. Company documents provided critical, virtually unlimited texts that expressed company language. Data within company files, on bulletin boards, and as documents-in-use such as policies conveyed the underlying company culture (Rapley, 2007). The company website and the content of associated 'pages' provided additional sources for textual analysis; numerous documents became part of the diverse collection of materials that helped address the three research questions (Rapley, 2007).

Observations. Angrosino stated ethnographers must use "all five senses when perceiving activities and interrelations of others in field settings" (as cited in Benedetto, 2009, p. 140). With any ethnography, observational research begins as soon as one enters the research environment. Before fieldwork could begin, several tools had to be in place to facilitate data collection: (a) a research map for the entire research period; (b) a plan for capturing notes electronically; (c) a template for gathering daily field notes; and (d) a system for converting field notes into a usable and easily understood form (Benedetto, 2009).

Detailed, descriptive field notes compiled extensive observations of daily work and interactions. During the course of seven weeks of direct observations, over 1600 digital images were collected to create visual records of employees performing tasks and responsibilities in all facets of company operations. These notes and images were critical elements during the analysis phase of the research.

Interviews and protocols. First-level interviews with company employees, leaders, founders, and customers included audio recordings to ensure verbatim accounts and accuracy in reporting. Interview protocols for each group varied slightly because of the types of questions asked. After recorded interviews were transcribed into a usable form, second-level interviews validated the transcriptions to ensure verbatim quotations and an accurate, unbiased reflection of expressed views and experiences of participants. Translations of some ESL interviews required the services of an outside bilingual transcriptionist who was bound by a Confidentiality Agreement and compensated by the researcher. Customer interviews were part of the research design to ascertain their views of company culture and the impact of character-based culture on employee interactions with customers.

Research Expansion

Research expanded beyond the initial design as the result of archival analysis. Adding interviews with two supplier representatives who contributed significantly to company success and with five members of the company advisory board who played key roles in the continuing development of the company was necessary to obtain a better perspective of company culture. A short, quantitative survey was developed and administered to part-time summer workers to assess personal preferences for working within the company.

MAJOR ASPECTS OF DATA ANALYSIS

Unlike other research methods where data analysis begins after completing data collection, ethnographic analysis involves three stages: Analysis in the field, immediate post-study analysis, and distance analysis. According to Benedetto (2009), "Ethnography is less precise than other qualitative research forms" (p. 151) that focuses on a single case or phenomenon. LeCompte and Schensul (1999a) noted a large volume of coded data must be condensed into "a concise collection of 'cooked' data collected over months of research" (as cited in Benedetto, 2009, p. 151). This condensation and synthesis are necessary to "achieve a deeper understanding of the culture under study" (Benedetto, 2009, p. 151). Thus, analysis within ethnographic research progresses concurrently with data collection.

Analysis in the Field

Field analysis involves recursive data analyses that include inscription, description, and transcription (Benedetto, 2009). The research questions were guideposts for observations, interviews, and archival research, but each day presented a unique set of work requirements, expectations, and experiences that did not exist the day before. According to Benedetto (2009), inscription involved making mental notes prior to writing things down as well as "learning to notice what others did not see" (p. 152).

Description included all processes whereby "notes, thoughts, ideas, and observations were captured from which 'thick descriptions,' narratives, interpretations, and explanations emerged and melded to create a holistic portrayal of the culture" (Benedetto, 2009, p. 152). "Thick" descriptions of daily life within the company required several explanatory pages. One described "how culinary and service teams acted like choreographed dance teams," [which resulted from visual images that] "enhanced the quality of the ethnography" (Benedetto, 2009, p. 149).

Transcription occurred off-site with the assistance of two paid transcribers bound by confidentiality agreements. They focused on creating accurate reproductions of recorded words, allowing the ethnographer to concentrate on "integrating data and the actual language used within the organization" (Benedetto, 2009, p. 153). After each week of research, "assessments of interactions over the course of the week determined if the research gained adequate observations" (Benedetto, 2009, p. 153) of all company areas defined in the research plan.

Immediate Post-Study Analysis

Tidying up, the coding philosophy, structure, and codebook, and computer-assisted qualitative data analysis comprised the elements of immediate post-study analysis. Tidying up included data cleaning, management, and cataloguing. Because of the volume of data collected daily within ethnographic research, these steps had to occur routinely and simultaneously with the research, unlike other research methods where these activities occur after data collection. Daily cleanup included such steps as arranging field notes and adding copied documents to the correct section of the field note binder. Weekly off-site cleanup included "cataloguing interviews and audiotapes according to the devised documentation management system" (Benedetto, 2009, p. 154).

Coding philosophy involved the inductive and deductive classification of data based on measurable, observable boundaries and at the lowest level of inference, i.e., where the ethnographer used concrete, commonly used descriptions of items. Coding helped "the classification process and the continued refinement of vast pieces of information into an understandable whole" (Benedetto, 2009, p. 154). The coding structure built on this philosophy and used concepts derived through interview construction, but some coding details did not emerge until research began to identify themes and patterns within observations and archival research (Benedetto, 2009). The codebook was essential in capturing all codes used in the analysis, the variables the codes represented, and the "kinds of items . . . coded for each variable" (LeCompte & Schensul, 1999a, p. 85).

Textual analysis is critical for understanding the language within any organization; fortunately, computer programs exist to assist in this formidable task. To perform this analysis effectively, a Microsoft-compatible program, MAXqda v.2, was used to display rich texts of all transcribed materials and develop hierarchical code lists from which coded texts could be more easily examined and linked (Benedetto, 2009). The advantage of MAXqda v.2 was its adaptability to both Dell and Apple platforms, both of which were used to support the study. MAXqda v.2 increased the dependability of interview narratives through the ready comparison of common threads, patterns, and themes that emerged from different perspectives evident in various interview texts.

Distance Analysis

The third stage of data analysis was the most robust and occurred after some time elapsed and field research had ended. Distance analysis "involved identifying patterns, analyzing structure, creating histories and summaries, creating a graphical conceptual framework, and describing the culture of the organization in a holistic sense" (Benedetto, 2009, p. 159). This stage took nearly seven weeks of intense structural, textual, and data analyses.

Benedetto (2009) noted structural analysis examined 11 specific areas, such as specific acts or behaviors, events, activities of a single event or longer settings, "strategies, practices, or tactics" [aimed at achieving a specific goal], "employee participation, involvement, and adaptation to specific settings," [and] "relationships and interactions between employees . . . and between employees and clients or customers" (p. 160). Textual analysis identified themes and topics within the company evident within "conversations, written words, phrases, and pictures" (Benedetto, 2009, p. 162). The brevity of this article prevents a detailed explanation of the social science approaches involved in textual analysis. Nonetheless, the reader should have a good understanding of the extensive nature of this specific ethnographic research study, from which business leaders continue to learn.

SUMMARY OF FINDINGS

Because qualitative research does not prove a hypothesis based on discrete, numerical data, critics have challenged the validity of interviews, labeling them as unscientific, subjective, and exploratory (Kvale, 2007). Yet interviews represent "a systematic investigation of knowledge . . . from which new knowledge emerges," (Kvale, as cited in Benedetto, 2009, p. 138), which supports the definition of science as "the methodical production of new, systematic knowledge" (p. 138). Similarly, when aligned with specific research questions and guided by a definitive research plan, observations of activities throughout an organization and archival research contribute to the body of knowledge and may constitute an entirely new field of study. Such was the case with the results of this study.

Rather than reiterate the results presented by Benedetto (2010), the following narrative provides a vignette of how ethnographic research has continued to drive change, growth, and success within the organization under study. The research revealed four cultural artifacts and three critical practices that emerged from the data and aligned to create the energy that fed organizational performance. Figure 1 depicts the model of these artifacts and practices that emerged from the research (Benedetto, 2010).

According to Benedetto (2009), "Each person brings his or her unique character into the workplace, where the traits of each person meld with others in a giant river of traits that represent the positive potential of the organization" (p. 414). This river of traits serves as the foundation from which organizational performance emerges. Within the study company, employees consistently demonstrated character through trust, caring, conscientiousness, respect, and a deep commitment to quality. Employees lived the core values of the organization, the first rules of which were doing what was moral, ethical, and legal, and always treating others with respect. Despite the multi-generational and cross-cultural aspects of the company, employees adhered to the values, with which customers and suppliers also identified and aligned.

Many stories emerged from the research about various aspects of company life, and all helped describe a culture of character. Ride-along observations with delivery personnel were especially exciting because observations of interactions with external customers revealed consistent application of core values by employees, which contributed to customer satisfaction, trust between customers and the company employees, and repeat business. Customers consistently stated they would not consider any other company as their catering source because they trusted company employees to deliver high-quality products exactly as ordered, on time, every time, which alleviated any anxiety about getting things done right. Employees epitomized the values of treating others with respect and providing quality in everything they did.

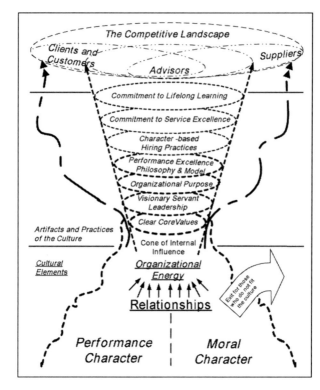

Figure 1. The Alignment of Cultural Artifacts and Practices as seen as a River of Character in Organizations.

IMPLICATIONS OF ETHNOGRAPHIC RESEARCH FOR AIDING BUSINESS PERFORMANCE

Business success and customer satisfaction depend on sustaining the delicate balance between delivering products and services to existing clients and feeding the production pipeline with new business (Benedetto, 2009). Thus, success results from disciplined individuals and teams that focus and direct efforts to create and sustain organizational energy (Benedetto, 2009). Leaders have the responsibility to define, shape, nurture, maintain, and sustain organizational culture (Schein, 2004). Thus, understanding organizational culture and its impact on organizational energy and performance is a critical leadership competence for company success. Understanding this culture and its impact on others can only be gained through ethnographic research.

Significant implications exist for all business leaders who can gain from studying the model that emerged from the research. First, organizational leaders need to see and understand the complexity and messiness of culture from a systemic perspective (Benedetto, 2009). Katzenbach and Harshak (2011) reinforced the need to understand the attitudes and behaviors that make a company powerful and cited at least one study that correlates strong, inspiring organizational cultures with financial results.

This study was no different on this account. Despite the economic downturn of recent years, the company continued to grow and add staff while showing strong financial performance. These results stem in part from universal commitment to lifelong learning, which includes open-book management practices, leadership development at all levels, and promotion of entrepreneurial activity within the company.

Second, company leaders need to assess and align employees and practices with core values as the critical first step before attempting any cultural transformation (Benedetto, 2009). Culture change requires work that some managers may be unwilling to invest unless the honesty and authenticity of company leaders is evident in action as well as words (Benedetto, 2009). To be successful, "Company leaders must be brutally honest in assessing the alignment of existing culture with the artifacts and practices defined by the study" (Benedetto, 2009, p. 432).

Third, the study validated the importance of character-based culture for the future success and sustainability of an enterprise. Small to mid-size companies were the primary targets of this study; implications exist for companies with fewer than 50 employees as well as those that employ between 50 and 200. Benedetto (2009) noted the value of this study for companies under 50 employees, especially family-run and family-owned businesses that are growing as well as those where leaders "may be stuck on how to get to the next level of performance" (p. 432). The study affirmed that "business leaders need to take stock of their own leadership styles, mentalities, and personalities to take their companies forward" (Benedetto, 2009, p. 432).

Fourth, regardless of company size, leaders need to act on building the seven foundational elements shown in Figure 1 to ensure business survival and sustainability, if these elements are not already in place. Company leaders need to assess their own leadership styles as well as the "styles of leaders throughout the organization to ensure consistency and alignment with core values" (Benedetto, 2009, p. 433). Alignment with core values is a priority with high-performing companies and determines, in part, how companies create strong reputations.

Benedetto (2009) noted "American business leaders are truly at crossroads [because] the public demands more accountability and stronger ethical performance from businesses, regardless of size" (p. 422). Leaders must realize that company culture is a valuable, critical element of their brand. As Bacon (2004) noted, customers are not fooled such that "leaders need to find the way toward rebuilding ethical corporate behaviors rooted in individual and corporate character that respects and honors the customer" (Benedetto, 2009, p. 422) as part of the company brand. This study showed how leaders have done just that through a character-based culture.

To summarize, "Leaders must accept and execute their responsibility to lead rather than simply manage," (Benedetto, 2009, p. 423) by engaging "moral character and higher levels of emotional intelligence" (p. 423) embodied within character-based culture The research concluded organizational culture helped drive the success of the company under study, and the "exceptional service, performance, and satisfaction among clients, customers, suppliers, advisers, leaders, and most of all, the employees through whom the company achieved success" (Benedetto, 2009, p. 423) were the results of that culture. These revelations would not have been possible without a detailed, ethnographic study as briefly described within this chapter.

CONCLUSION

This chapter addressed the design and execution of an effective 2009 ethnographic study that revealed artifacts and practices within a character-based culture and how artifacts and practices combined to drive exceptional company performance. The comparison of different qualitative research methods showed how ethnographic research is the best research method for understanding company culture. The introduction of ethnographic methods within a business culture and the short discussions on the major aspects of data collection and analysis intended to frame the critical details that led to a successful study.

Because of space limitations, the cultural model that emerged from the research was the only element brought forward to summarize study results. Readers are encouraged to examine Benedetto (2010) for more details. The chapter concluded with some implications of ethnographic research for aiding business performance.

Some researchers have shied away from ethnographic research because of the time involved in designing, executing, and completing studies of this nature. Unlike other studies that focus on a limited aspect of organizational experience, ethnographic research provides a unique opportunity to examine the systemic nature of company life and the dynamics that arise through spontaneous human interactions. No other research form provides this opportunity.

Benedetto (2009) noted how the study yielded "an optimal experience because the company presented constant stimulation and demonstrations of psychic energy" (p. 637) that had "mental, physical, psychological, and emotional dimensions" (p. 637). The total consumption of the researcher within an ethnographic study can be overwhelming or liberating. The research can be overwhelming if one attempts to control every aspect of the study, but it can be liberating as one becomes accustomed to being "in the moment" of direct observations, much as a fly on the wall flits from point to point while maintaining a guiding purpose for each movement or observation.

Through the short but pointed discussions within this chapter, the reader should have a better understanding of the purpose and design of ethnographic study. Rather than being daunting, the magnitude of ethnographic study should be seen as an opportunity to apply the full depth of qualitative research to specific environments through which researchers and leaders can gain new insight and knowledge. The purpose of this specific ethnographic study was to help leaders understand company culture to improve performance and outcomes; this objective was achieved and affirmed through the formal recognition awarded the study.

REFERENCES

Addison, R. B. (1989). Grounded interpreted research: An investigation of physician socialization. In M. J. Parker & R. B. Addison (Eds.), *Entering the circle: Hermeneutic investigation in psychology* (pp. 39–57). New York, NY: SUNY Press.

Agar, M. H. (1986). *Speaking of ethnography.* Newbury Park, CA: Sage Publications, Inc.

Angrosino, M. (2007). *Doing ethnographic and observational research* (1st ed.). Thousand Oaks, CA: Sage Publications, Inc.

Argandoña, A. (2003). Fostering values in organizations. *Journal of Business Ethics, 45*(1/2, Part 2), 15–28.

Atkinson, P. (1992). *Understanding ethnographic texts.* Newbury Park, CA: Sage Publications, Inc.

Atkinson, P., Coffey, A., Delamont, S., Lofland, J., & Lofland, L. (Eds.). (2007). *Handbook of Ethnography* (1st ed.). Thousand Oaks, CA: Sage Publications, Inc.

Bacon, T. (2004). You are how you behave: Customers can't be fooled. *Journal of Business Strategy, 25*(4), 35–40.

Benedetto, R. L. (2009). An ethnographic study of character-based culture in a small business setting (Doctoral dissertation). Retrieved from ProQuest Dissertations and Theses. (UMI 3394574)

Benedetto, R. L. (2010). The power of the river of character in organizations. In C. Lentz (Ed.). *Refractive thinker volume IV: Ethics, leadership and globalization* (pp. 103–134). Las Vegas, NV: Refractive Thinker© Press.

Bowen, S. A. (2004, July). Organizational factors encouraging ethical decision making: An exploration into the case of an exemplar. *Journal of Business Ethics, 52*(4), 311–324.

Chun, R. (2005). Ethical character and virtue of organizations: An empirical assessment and strategic implications. *Journal of Business Ethics, 57*(3), 269–284.

Clandinin, D. J., & Connelly, F. M. (2000). *Narrative inquiry: Experience and story in qualitative research.* San Francisco, CA: Jossey-Bass.

Collins, J., & Porras, J. (1994). *Built to last.* New York, NY: Harper Business.

Cone, J. D., & Foster, S. L. (1999). *Dissertations and theses from start to finish: Psychology and related fields.* Washington, DC: American Psychological Association.

Coulon, A. (1995). *Ethnomethodology.* Thousand Oaks, CA: Sage Publications, Inc.

Creswell, J. W. (2003). *Research design: Qualitative, quantitative, and mixed methods approaches.* Thousand Oaks, CA: Sage Publications, Inc.

Dickson, M. W., Smith, D. B., Grojean, M. W., & Ehrhart, M. (2001). An organizational climate regarding ethics: The outcome of leader values and the practices that reflect them. *The Leadership Quarterly, 12*(2), 197–217.

Grojean, M. W., Resick, C. J., Dickson, M. W., & Smith, D. B. (2004). Leaders, values, and organizational climate: Examining leadership strategies for establishing an organizational climate regarding ethics. *Journal of Business Ethics, 55*(3), 223–241.

Hitt, W. D. (1990). *Ethics and leadership: Putting theory into practice* (1st ed.). Columbus, OH: Batelle Press.

Jones, A. M. (2006, June). Culture, identity, and motivation: The historical anthropology of a family firm. *Culture and Organization, 2*(2), 169–183.

Katzenbach, J., & Harshak, A. (2011, Spring). Stop blaming your culture. *Strategy+business, 62,* 34–43.

Key, S. (1999). Organizational ethical climate: Real or imagined? *Journal of Business Ethics, 20*(3), 217–225.

Kvale, S. (2007). *Doing interviews.* (1st ed.). Thousand Oaks, CA: Sage Publications, Inc.

LeCompte, M. D., & Schensul, J. J. (1999a). *Analyzing and interpreting ethnographic data* (1st ed.). Walnut Creek, CA: AltaMira Press.

LeCompte, M. D., & Schensul, J. J. (1999b). *Designing and conducting ethnographic research* (1st ed.). Walnut Creek, CA: AltaMira Press.

Lincoln, Y. S., & Guba, E. G. (1985). *Naturalistic inquiry.* Newbury Park, CA: Sage Publications, Inc.

Maheshwari, S. K., & Ganesh, M. P. (2006, April-June). Ethics in organizations: The case of Tata Steel. *Vikalpa: The Journal for Decision-makers, 31*(2), 75–87.

Meglino, B. M., & Ravlin, E. C. (1998). Individual values in organizations: Concepts, controversies, and research. *Journal of Management, 24*(3), 351–389.

Moustakas, C. (1994). *Phenomenological research methods.* Thousand Oaks, CA: Sage Publications, Inc.

Patton, M. (1990). *Qualitative evaluation and research methods.* Newbury Park, CA: Sage Publications.

Rapley, T. (2007). *Doing conversation, discourse, and document analysis.* (1st ed.). Thousand Oaks, CA: SAGE Publications, Inc. Publications, Inc.

Schein, E. H. (2004). *Organizational culture and leadership.* (3rd ed.). San Francisco, CA: Jossey-Bass.

Schneider, B. (1987). The people make the place. *Personnel Psychology, 40*(3), 437–453.

Schwartzman, H. B. (1993). *Ethnography in organizations.* Newbury Park, CA: Sage Publications, Inc.

Spradley, J. (1980). *Participant observation.* New York, NY: Holt, Rinehart, & Winston.

Stewart, A. (1998). *The ethnographer's method.* Thousand Oaks, CA: Sage Publications, Inc.

Van Maanen, J. (1982). Fieldwork on the beat. In J. Van Maanen, J. M. Dabbs, & R. R. Faulkner (Eds.), *Varieties of qualitative research* (pp. 103–151). Beverly Hills, CA: Sage Publications, Inc.

About the Author

Dr. Ramon L. (Ray) Benedetto, or Dr. Ray as he is known to his students, is a scholar-practitioner who holds accredited degrees from Penn State (Bachelor of Science, Health Planning and Administration), the University of Southern California (Master of Science, Systems Management), and University of Phoenix (Doctor of Management, Organizational Leadership). He also holds numerous diplomas from military schools and programs. Dr. Ray teaches leadership, management, and strategic planning and implementation for the University of Phoenix MBA Program at the Chicago Campus. A Distinguished Military Graduate of the Air Force ROTC program at Penn State, Dr. Ray served on active duty for nearly 25 years, rising to the rank of Colonel before returning to civilian life. Dr. Ray leads a consulting firm that focuses on organizational transformation and helps leaders build high-performing, character-based organizations.

Dr. Ray is board certified in healthcare management and a Fellow of the American College of Healthcare Executives where he serves as a mentor. He is also an active member of the Academy of Management and serves as an academic reviewer and program contributor. He is currently working on a book about character-based business with leaders of several companies.

The University of Phoenix recognized Dr. Ray's dissertation, *An Ethnographic Study of Character-based Culture in a Small Business Setting,* as the 2010 Qualitative Dissertation of the Year. He published *The Power of the River of Character in Organizations* in Volume IV *of the Refractive Thinker®*.

To reach Dr. Ray for more information, please e-mail: ray@guidestarinc.com

QUALITATIVE

CHAPTER 4

A Qualitative Examination: Ways of Leading Among Non-Profit Executives

Dr. Gillian Silver

Non-profit organizations have been neglected in current research and inadequately explored to determine what kind of leadership is present. This chapter addresses the research methodology applied The 2008 Silver Study, *A Qualitative Examination: Ways of Leading Among Non-Profit Executives* which focused specifically on expressions of the lived experiences of seasoned executives. Context-bound, holistic reflections sought the emergence of themes assessed through content analysis. In doing so, this journey revealed characteristics that are commonly held among those profiled, and suggested what non-profit leadership *looks like.* By considering the perspectives of those who both modeled character and met the financial expectations of their organizations, key conclusions were drawn which can be considered for Transfer into third sector environments, where a leadership deficit is being experienced, and expected to intensify through 2040.

This study used a total of 30 interviews with 10 participants, implemented through a series of three in-depth interviews, as advocated by Seidman (1998). The structured and carefully developed outreach explored the question of how leader philosophy and behavior are exhibited among non-profit leaders situated in a common geographic area. Copies of the interview questions, procedures, transcriptions, and key study support evidence can be found in the appendix of the original work.

Pratt and Foreman's (2000) definition of the qualitative research approach served as the foundation for the 2008 Silver Study, which also relied on an iterative data gathering process. Similarly, Creswell (2002) contends that "qualitative research is used to study research problems requiring an exploration and understanding of a central phenomenon" (p. 50). A qualitative investigation was important to this study because of the depth of subject experience, and the potential for transfer of the findings (Byrne, 2001; Farber, 2006; Oakley, 2004; Ponterotto, 2005; Rennie, 2002). As noted by Weiss (2004) "Qualitative interviews ask about the details of what happened: what was done and said, what the respondent thought and felt" (p. 44). Weiss (2004) stated "the aim is to come as close as possible to capturing in full the processes that led to an event or experience" (p. 44). The 2008 Silver Study subsequently presented a densely detailed description of what happened, and extended a basis for a theory of "why it happened" (p. 44). The qualitative investigation considered the experiences and perspectives of the participants. The search for the voice of those studied is reflective of "a human science that is guided by a synthesis of meaning essences" (Moustakas, 1994, p. 41). He contends the search for expression represents "natural processes through which awareness, understanding, and knowledge are derived" (p. 41).

Seidman's (1998) work provided the pattern for the multipart qualitative phenomenological interviews. Further, the inquiry employed inductive data analysis techniques combined with the data comparison and classification processes. This process supported an in-depth review of the participants' commentary and relevancy to the dissertation focus. Dym and Hutson (2006) contends that investigating leadership through observation and study is theoretically sound as "the idea that individuals and the context in which they live reciprocally influence one another has become a commonplace of social science research. The power of person-context interaction is so great that it literally shapes all levels of human behavior" (p.

69). By examining lived experience, the researcher gains insight into the individual's decision-making, and the patterns of their conduct.

THE PERTINENCE OF A QUALITATIVE STUDY OF NON-PROFIT LEADERSHIP BEHAVIORS

There will be enormous demand for leaders in the nonprofit environments of the future. Anticipated organizational requirements include the need for competency in executive positions in light of impending Baby Boomer departures, increased external scrutiny of non-profit management and financial administration, and potentially more lucrative employment opportunities for individuals favoring corporate positions rather than affiliation with civic, social, educational, or membership-oriented non-profits.

A qualitative methodology offered distinct advantages for the researcher to explore experiences that were holistic, context-bound, and personal in their viewpoint (Leedy & Ormrod, 2001; Shank, 2002). As articulated by Wilson (2002), a phenomenological study examines human phenomena without assessing the related causes or appearances. The principal ambition is to consider how human phenomena are experienced in consciousness, and in cognitive and perceptual acts. This may lead to an understanding of how the experiences are valued or aesthetically appreciated (Wilson, 2002). Similarly, Creswell (2002) states that "qualitative research is used to study research problems requiring an exploration and understanding of a central phenomenon" (p. 50). A qualitative investigation was important to this study because of the depth of subject experience that was revealed, and the potential for transfer of the findings (Byrne, 2001; Donalek 2005; Farber, 2006; Manen, 1990; Oakley, 2004; Patton, 2002; Ponterotto, 2005; Rennie, 2002). As noted by Weiss (2004), "Qualitative interviews ask about the details of what happened: what was done and said, what the respondent thought and felt" (p.44). Weiss (2004) stated that "the aim is to come as close as possible to capturing in full the processes that led to an event or experience. Of particular note was, that "In-depth interviews can provide vivid descriptions of personal experience . . . They are the best source of information about people's thoughts and feelings and the motives and emotions that lead them to act as they do" (Weiss, 2004, p. 45). There is agreement in the literature that qualitative research can provide rich descriptions and help construct an understanding of the social world, according to many in the qualitative methodology realm, including Denzin and Lincoln (2000, p. 488).

There are four distinct phases in qualitative research, according to Makowski and Stein (2004). The first involves the act of asking, the second, witnessing, the third interpreting, and finally, the act of knowing. Makowski and Stein (2004) describe the function of exploring through asking as a necessary step in recognizing the metaphors and assumptions of experience. When witnessing, the researcher gains first-hand access to the experience of the subject, and this provides an engaged aspect to the qualitative research process. Interpreting, as explained by Makowski and Stein (2004), enables the potential conceptualization of the meaning of the subjects' experiences as conveyed to the researcher. Finally, the last phase allows for the isolation of common themes of experience that contribute to field knowledge, and potentially, an insightful interpretation of the subject's experience. In reviewing the nature of their professional choices, novice leaders may gain insight into best practices they too can apply in the third sector.

Seidman's (1998) work provided an appropriate pattern for multipart qualitative phenomenological interviews. This design "involves conducting a series of three separate interviews with each participant [so that] . . . people's behavior becomes meaningful and understandable when placed in the context of their lives and the lives around them" (p. 11). The first interview concentrated on acquiring relevant background on the subject and serves as a focused life history. Seidman (1998) said, "The interviewer's task is to put the participant's experience in context by asking him or her to tell as much as possible about him or herself in light of the topic up to the present time" (p. 11). The discussion is generally restricted to 90 minutes to ensure depth in interaction but a consistency among the interview set. The second interview explored what Seidman called "the details of the experience" (p. 12). Respondents are intentionally not asked for opinions, "but rather the details of their experience, upon which their opinions may be built" (p. 12). The researcher intentionally encourages reflection, rather than editorialization, to ensure that the interview subject is deeply considering the implications of their behavioral choices.

In the final interview, "participants are asked to reflect on the meaning of their experience; it addresses the intellectual and emotional connections between the participants' work and life" (p. 12). This component is a point of integration as "making sense or meaning requires that the participants look at how the factors in their lives interacted to bring them to their present situation" (p. 12). This approach enables the study to present conclusions with specific and, possibly, shared language.

THEORETICAL FOUNDATION

Conducting and recording of comprehensive interviews provided data for the subsequent identification of categories that can be expressed as themes. In-depth phenomenological interviewing provides merit when examining how subjects have come to reach key conclusions about their lives and behavior. Perhaps the most distinguishing of all its features, the model of in-depth phenomenological interviewing applied in this study involved conducting a series of three separate interviews with each participant. Behavior becomes meaningful and understandable when placed in the context of their lives and the lives of those around them (Seidman,

1998, p. 11). Without context, the literature suggests there is little possibility of exploring the meaning of an experience (Melanson, 2004; Patton, 1989). "Qualitative approaches are particularly useful for understanding the nuances of the ways—understanding people's thought processes, decision framework, and emotional motivations—as opposed to the more tangible how many's (*sic*) and which one's (*sic*)," states Melanson (2004, p. 26). Further, this methodology enables the researcher to gain specific insight into personal perspective and the dimensions that influenced professional choices. Yet another benefit is the opportunity for personal philosophies to emerge in the discussion.

Two criteria determine the number of participants in a study reliant on in-depth phenomenological interviews, according to Seidman (1998). He identified the first as sufficiency: "Are there sufficient numbers to reflect the range of participants and sites that make up the population so that others outside the sample might have a chance to connect to the experiences of those in it?" (pp. 47–48). The second criterion is saturation of information. Seidman (1998) explained that he would be reluctant to establish a particular number. "*Enough* is an interactive reflection of every step of the interview process and different for each study and each researcher" (p. 48). He suggested that researchers know when there are enough participants when they cease to discover anything new.

RESEARCH PROCESS

Qualitative methods were appropriate to the study because of their ability to describe subjective and experientially based reflections (Creswell, 1994; Merriam, 1998; Patton, 2002; Wilson, 2002; Whitley & Crawford, 2005). Seidman (1998) argued that multiple-step interviews are particularly valuable when deciding upon methodology selection and applicability.

The purpose of in-depth interviewing is not to get answers to questions, nor to test hypothesis, and not to *evaluate* as the term is normally used. Siedman (1998) contends that at the root of in-depth interviewing is an interest in expanding the experience of other people and the meaning they make of that experience (p. 3). Qualitative approaches do not begin with a theoretical foundation that is tested or verified, but theory may emerge from the process of gathering and analyzing the research data. This expectation is appropriate to anticipate as theories or patterns are likely to emerge in design because the specific intent of the study is not to be a work constrained by a theory (Creswell, 1994), but one that brings new dimension to the findings and to the overall body of knowledge. Creswell (1994) states qualitative research studies involve the collection of data "consisting of words (i.e., text) from participants during interview" (p. 43). This form of inquiry analyzes words "by describing events and deriving themes," [asking broad questions but suspending judgment by making no predictions and relying instead on participants] "to shape what they report" (Creswell, 1994, p. 44). Through the identification of common interpretations and semantics, the researcher can isolate commonalities in thinking, and draw comparisons in regards to potential best practices.

An orientation inherent to qualitative research is that it "is not looking for principles that are true all the time and in all conditions . . . rather, the goal is understanding of specific circumstances, how and why things actually happen in a complex world" (Rubin & Rubin, 1995, p. 38). Larger understandings emerge from the recognition that "knowledge in qualitative interviewing is situational and conditional. The underlying assumption is that if you cannot understand something in the specific first, you cannot understand in the general later" (p. 38). Each interview subject will address questions from a personal framework, but when viewed collectively, the responses reveal deeper understandings and, perhaps, similarity in perspective.

The literature suggests there is particular merit in qualitative research as it uses interview questions that go deeper than traditional survey responses or quickly completed inquiry instruments. The use of unstructured questions also often elicits high-caliber results. Weiss (2004) noted that "questions are usually formulated during the interview rather than written out beforehand. There are no magic phrasings which will reliably elicit illuminating responses" (p. 46). Weiss (2004) suggested that "concrete observation, combined with the respondent's sometimes generalized responses, can lead to more full and accurate reports of the exchange" (p. 47). When assessed during the data analysis stage, the findings can potentially be deep rather than narrow, and document what Capra (1996) defines as interconnections and collaborations in the web of life.

Application of a legitimate model for qualitative interviews relies on the recognition that "we are trying to find in detail how the conversational partners understand what they have seen, heard, or experienced. We want to elicit from conversational partners examples, narratives, histories, stories, and explanations" (Rubin & Rubin, 1995, p. 40). The overall intention culminates, explained Weiss (1994), in a set of examined topics which constitute the study's "substantive frame" (p. 15).

APPROPRIATENESS OF DESIGN

As the qualitative study required Silver to situate herself within the 2008 inquiry, concerns could be raised about the objectivity of the exploration. Certain requirements exist to ensure that in reviewing their familiarity with the material and phenomenon under study, "personal biases, values, and assumptions" (Creswell, 2003, p. 49) are reported. From a standpoint of advantages, this form of research speaks to "data collection procedures in which inquirers are sensitive to participants, actively collaborate with them (rather than studying them), and respect the dignity of each individual who offers data for research" (p. 49). Caution is needed to ensure that respondents have the opportunity to answer the questions without being led, and to wander as their reach their conclusions. In this way, the interview process becomes a vital element of the investigation itself.

Care must be given to the manner in which interview questions are formulated, as improper articulation can taint interpretation and skew results. "There are two key principles . . . avoid confusion and keep the respondents' perspective in mind" (Neuman, 2003, p. 268). Neuman (2003) addressed how the interviewer is to recognize the inherent value of the respondents' experiences and understanding level. While it is not possible to speak to each person with equal clarity and "tailoring question wording to each respondent makes comparisons almost impossible" (Neuman, p. 269), a researcher must recognize that "question writing is more of an art than a science. It takes skill, practice, patience, and creativity" (p. 269). Rubin and Rubin (1995) observed that variances in approach and intent exist throughout the formal qualitative interview process. During the early stages of research, "the interview serves to gather themes and ideas" (p. 46). As the discussions advance and subsequent interviews are conducted with the same subject, research efforts begin to focus on a limited number of themes, while "in the final stages, you emphasize more the analysis and testing of your understanding as you put themes together, begin to form theories, and run them by your interviewees and critical readers in your field" (p. 46). Similarly, Seidman (1998) encouraged a multiple-part approach to qualitative interview design. This "model of in-depth phenomenological interviewing involves conducting a series of three separate interviews with each participant [so that] . . . people's behavior becomes meaningful and understandable when placed in the context of their lives and the lives around them" (p. 11).

The first interview concentrated on acquiring relevant background on the subject and serves as a focused life history. Seidman (1998) said, "The interviewer's task is to put the participant's experience in context by asking him or her to tell as much as possible about him or herself in light of the topic up to the present time" (p. 11). The second interview explores what Seidman (1998) called "the details of the experience" (p.12). Participants were asked for "the details of their experience, upon which their opinions may be built" (p. 12).

In the final interview, "participants are asked to reflect on the meaning of their experience; it addresses the intellectual and emotional connections between the participants' work and life" (Siedman, 1998, p. 12). This last step functions as a point of integration as "making sense or meaning requires that the participants look at how the factors in their lives interacted to bring them to their present situation" (p. 12). This approach enabled the study to present conclusions with specific and possibly shared language. The three-part interview process relied on unstructured questions that were built from one discussion to the next. After each set of interviews, the data were coded and analyzed. Following each phase, the analyzed data were used to shape the questions for the subsequent unstructured interview in the series. Collectively, the multiple-step approach captured detail that offers reflections and sharper correlations among respondents.

RESEARCH TOPIC

The selected research topic, the exploration of the ways of leadership among non-profit leaders, is of importance both to those who operate in this sector and to those who benefit from the social system contributions of the nation's non-profit organizations. Changing economic conditions, challenges in maintaining competent team members, and increasing costs are just some of the comprehensive issues impacting 501(c) 3 organizations. The literature suggested that further turbulence is ahead as non-profit boards and trustees struggle to replace their retiring Baby Boomer executives (Millar, 1990; Tierney, 2004).

The 2008 Silver Study is relevant as the conclusions have the potential to positively influence leader performance and operational decision-making. The research has particular value for emerging leadership, as the study population concentrated on seasoned executives, exclusively senior-level leaders with an average of 21.4 years of direct service in the non-profit sector. The interview subjects provided distinctive articulations of leadership experience and reflections that are of potential merit to less tenured non-profit managers. The intention and content focus of the 2008 Silver Study called for development of research situated in the many perspectives of the evolving nature of leadership. The literature review supporting the study is comprehensive. Gardner's (1993, 1995, 1999, 2007) multiple intelligences construct and Goleman's (1995, 2005, 2006) theory of emotional intelligence create a frame for the examination of the many dimensions of leadership. Further, theories that are significant to the non-profit sector, such as Servant leadership (Greenleaf & Spears, 2002), and stewardship (Blanchard & Hodges, 2003), are incorporated.

POPULATION

The overall target population for this study consisted of executives based in metropolitan Las Vegas, Nevada, operating in non-profit organizations classified by the United States Internal Revenue Service as 501(c) 3. These leaders represented a variety of mission-driven groups including health and human services and arts, civic, religious, and educational organizations. While there was some anticipated variance in the position titles and key accountabilities among the participants, each was identified because he or she holds senior manager status, with most being executive directors.

The interview pool was selected from a group of prequalified subjects based on the evaluation of the complete Las Vegas non-profit organization population as compiled by the Volunteer Center of Nevada list of 300-plus organizations. Multiple criteria were applied to the target population to make certain that the interview population was qualified. The first criterion applied was that the organization with whom the leader is affiliated must be a 501(c)3 non-profit. It had to be considered successful as measured by the American Institute for Philanthropy and the Better Business Bureau's Wise Giving Alliance. The final criterion was the leader possessed a minimum of 10 years of non-profit experience. This approach to population identification is purposeful sampling, as advocated by Whitley and Crawford (2005), Creswell (2003) and Leedy and Ormrod (2001). The intention was to select study participants based on the projected relevance of their experience.

SAMPLING FRAME

The first of the three-part interview process consisted of a meeting in person with prequalified participants serving as leaders within metropolitan Las Vegas non-profit organizations. This stage in the investigation provided insight into the participant's professional background and leadership philosophies. Additionally, this interview was used to validate the subject's background to ensure that the respondent met the study requirements. If a potential participant did not meet the requirements, procedures were in place to identify an additional participant to replace the one who was dropped from the study.

The initial interview also served to explain in more detail the purpose and time commitment required of the volunteers. Further, the first semi-structured discussion provided them with the opportunity to acceptor decline participation in the rest of the interviewing process. Initially, it was projected that ideally, the study would focus on seasoned leaders with a minimum of 10 years' experience in non-profit organizations. Seasoned leadership was chosen so that only those individuals who had truly developed their leadership style were included.

CONFIDENTIALITY

This study was executed so that both privacy and confidentiality of all participants were protected. Consent forms did not incorporate private information, and the responses of subjects were not discussed with other respondents. All of the proceedings involved in the study were recorded for later transcription to enable accurate coding procedures. The identity of the participants remained confidential. Additionally, the confidentiality of the data sets was maintained and not shared among respondents, except in the form of generalized conclusions.

A coding and tracking system was applied to all results to ensure that appropriate follow-up steps were taken to encourage participation. All results provided within the body of the dissertation and in any subsequent journal articles, books, or lectures were presented in generalizations to protect the identity of study participants. Further, from the standpoint of ethical execution, the 2008 Silver Dissertation Study conformed to Meltzoff's (1998) view of diligence in every aspect of design and execution. He stated, "Ethical standards apply at every point along the way, including the choice of criteria measures and how they were applied, how the data were analyzed, how the graphics were portrayed, what generalizations were made, and what conclusions and inferences were drawn" (p. 147). The researcher must strive for consistency in all practices, so any form of possible distortion, or premature conclusion, is avoided prior to the analysis of the content and identification of themes.

To ensure integrity, all interviews were recorded and archived so the original data were maintained. Additionally, all methods used to manipulate the data and draw conclusions were documented either in the body of the dissertation or were included in attachments to the dissertation. This information was archived along with the original interviews. The participants were asked a variety of questions during the interview series as they were guided through a process of inquiry. The documentation and audio recording process was the same in all interviews. Follow-up calls were made for each interview to confirm participation interest and appointment details. The interviews took place in the participants' offices.

RESEARCH STUDY SEQUENCE

The research methods for this qualitative study incorporated a series of sequences. The steps were as follows:

1. Perform a literature review to evaluate the evolution of leadership theory and emotional intelligence and to develop interview questions that will access the association of this material with leaders in non-profit settings.

2. Identify the target population of non-profit leaders residing in metropolitan Las Vegas, Nevada.

3. Isolate the research population by conducting screening interviews with organizational leaders identified through referral or those who are included in the metropolitan nonprofit list provided by the Volunteer Center of Southern Nevada.

4. Complete the first interview in the three-part series. The intention is to gather biographical and historical information on the subject.

5. Transcribe the interviews.

6. Code the data, using personal analysis via the Transana diagnostic software program.

7. Identify properties within the data.

8. Analyze the data, isolating themes and descriptions.

9. Refine the questions that will guide the second unstructured interview.

10. Complete the second interview in the three-part series. The intention is to solicit experience-based reflections on leadership.

11. Transcribe the interviews.

12. Code the data, using personal analysis via the Transana analysis software program.

13. Identify properties within the data.

14. Analyze the data, isolating themes and descriptions.

15. Refine the questions that will guide the third unstructured interview.

16. Complete the third and final interview in the series. The intention is to explore how the non-profit leader will bridge experience to leadership behavior and future decisions.

17. Transcribe the interviews.

18. Code the data, using personal analysis via the Transana diagnostic software program.

19. Identify properties within the data.

20. Analyze the data, isolating themes and descriptions.

21. Report the conclusions.

22. Store the data.

Application of this comprehensive sequence of activities ensured that the 2008 Silver Study was in compliance with the highest principles of qualitative research.

INTERVIEW

The primary instrumentation for data collection exercised in the 2008 Silver Study was the interview. Three phases were used: the first served to gather background information on the participants such as why they were attracted to the non-profit environment and what drove them to remain employed within this sector. The second interview examined current reflections on non-profit leadership and leadership characteristics. The third interview concentrated on the participants' intentions to shape their future leadership choices and their awareness of the sustaining characteristics needed to thrive in non-profit environments. Probing questions were developed to support each component of the three-interview process. Additionally, the content analysis, coding and subsequent identification of themes emerging from the first interview were incorporated in the second interview. The third interview incorporated themes that emerged from the second interview.

STUDY DESIGN

The 2008 Silver Study relied on 30 one-on-one interviews with 10 seasoned non-profit leaders. The unstructured questioning strategy advocated by Dicicco-Bloom and Crabtree (2006) was used. This method was used with a specified respondent field of qualified representatives in executive positions in the targeted geographic market.

DATA COLLECTION

This section of the article serves to clarify the process by which respondents were identified and the manner in which the data were gathered, organized, and prepared for final analysis in the formal study. The steps in qualitative data collection process were defined by Creswell (2002) as follows:

- Obtaining permission to conduct the study, selecting participants and sites purposefully to best understand the phenomenon, identifying data from various sources such as observations, interviews, documents, audio-visual materials, administering and recording data using protocols, such as observational and interview protocols, and then administering the data collection in a manner sensitive to individuals and sites (Creswell, 2002, p. 191).

- Two primary approaches were employed in the study. The first was unstructured interviews "consisting of asking a few, open-ended questions and recording the views and meaning of participant interviews" (Creswell, 2002, p. 199). The second approach was "unstructured observational data consisting of observing and taking field notes or constructing drawings about a setting," (Creswell, 2002, p. 199).

- Field notes, "text (words) recorded by the researcher during an observation in a qualitative study" (Creswell, 2002, p. 201) were maintained throughout the interview process. This served to "record a description of the events, activities, and people (e.g., what happened)" and to capture "personal thoughts that researchers have that relate to their insights, hunches, or broad ideas or themes that emerge during the observation" (p. 203).

The identified participants were contacted by telephone to explain the nature of the study and to request a brief meeting as part of the screening process. The participants were validated against the target population screening process mentioned earlier in this article. When the prospective participant and their organizations met these qualifications, they were asked to volunteer for this study. Those individuals who agreed to participate were then scheduled for the first in-person interview, which served as the start of the formal data collection process. To prepare for the discussion, the potential participant received a packet containing the following elements: a cover letter requesting his or her participation in the study, the informed consent form, and information on the multiple-part interview process.

Specific procedures for the interview process, as informed by the work of Creswell (2002), were as follows: "Identify the interviewees. . . . Determine the type of interview. . . . Audio-tape the questions and responses. . . . Take brief notes during the interview. . . . Use probes (sub questions) to obtain additional information" (pp. 207–208). Transcription enabled conversion of the "field notes into text data" (Creswell, 2002, p. 259). This allowed the subsequent assembly of a preliminary exploratory analysis evolving from a "general sense of the data" (Creswell, 2002, p. 265). These steps were supported by data recording protocols which captured detail for later analysis.

DATA ANALYSIS

Once acquired, the interview responses were analyzed to identify results and to isolate shared variables, patterns, or any other consistencies that exist among the respondents. The purpose was to examine ways of leading among non-profit leaders. It was further projected that results would be compared with the data gathered from the literature review process. Data were coded according to the process outlined by Creswell (2002). The codes reflect the recommendations of Bogdan and Bilken (1998) by isolating setting, context, and perspectives. Themes, "similar codes aggregated together to form a major idea in the database" (Creswell, year, p.

267), were isolated and broken into the following categories: major themes, minor themes, and potential themes. Descriptions, "a detailed rendering of people, places or events" (Creswell, 2002, p. 267), were drawn and provided for layered themes and sequencing of ideas. The following steps were employed to explore and build upon themes: 1) dialogue that provides support for themes; 2) use metaphors and analogies; 3) collect quotes from interview data; 4) locate multiple perspectives and contrary evidence; 5) look for vivid detail, identify tensions and contradictions in individual experiences; 6) create a visual image of the information in the form of a comparison table; and 7) describe personal or demographic information on each subject (Creswell, 1994, pp. 276–277).

Once the data were collected, codes were attached to the data to reflect the initial analysis, and a more in-depth assessment was completed. The findings were then interpreted. This served to isolate parallels and enabled the formation of "some larger meaning about the phenomenon based on personal views and/or comparisons with past studies" (Creswell, 1994, pp. 277–278). The information was assessed, as advocated by Creswell (1994, 2002) to establish dimension and parallels relevant to the focus of the descriptive exploration. The study population was defined in terms of demographics with a graphical presentation incorporated into the final academic product. Creswell (2002) advocated the process of member checking, during which study participants are asked to "check the accuracy of the account" which involves asking if "the description is complete and realistic, if the themes are accurate, and if the interpretations are fair and representative of those that can be made" (p. 280).

INTERNAL THREATS

Internal threats to the validity of the three-interview process included the possibility that an element of subjectivity existed in the phrasing of the questions. A secondary internal threat was the possible isolation of key words that may have had meaning beyond the context of the study.

SUMMARY

Because of the nature of the non-profit executive and the increasing pressure to generate higher levels of funds through community outreach sponsorships, signature projects, and donations, it was anticipated based on the results of initial exploratory discussions that some potential participants would be uneasy with the use of a 360-degree assessment—a tool commonly applied in an identification process. In a strictly qualitative study supported by primary research, respondents can experience greater comfort in one-on-one interviews. The study's exploratory and descriptive approach was not intended to develop or disprove specific theories but to build, as advocated by Creswell (1994), details that offer the opportunity for abstraction and concepts.

Qualitative interviewing allows the acquisition of different points of view. As Rubin and Rubin (1995) stated, "Getting one side of an argument is not sufficient. You have to go for balance in your choice of interviews to represent all the divisions within the arena of study" (p. 69). The use of multiple interviews with the sample populations and the selection of participants from non-profits of varying size, sophistication, and mission focus allowed for a larger view of the nature of leadership in these settings. Additionally, as noted by (Simon & Frances, 2002), qualitative methodology supports the view that the world is holistic and that no single reality exists among all individuals. By seeking meaning and purpose, as expressed through experience and philosophy, understanding of the qualifications of current-day nonprofit leaders can be used to inform the selection of their replacements.

In the selection of germinal and other supporting literature the study reflected a content review which was, by nature, a subjective process. It was, therefore, vulnerable to perception and subsequent interpretation. Content analysis has been defined as a systematic compression of many words of text into fewer content categories (Stemler, 2003). It offers the researcher a process for the actual collection and assessment of textural material. Neuman (2003) noted its flexibility and value as a far-reaching analysis approach that examines both the primary message and latent content, such as the symbolic meaning attached to words or phrases. He stated that content refers to "words, meanings, pictures, symbols, ideas, themes, or any message that can be communicated" (p. 310).

As this study applied pure research to the business world, the 2008 Silver Study functions as an example of applied descriptive research. This form of research is defined as qualitative, and its stated purpose in this study was to examine leadership behavior among non-profit executives. Both the merits and drawbacks of qualitative research were addressed in the literature review. As addressed previously, the researcher intended to examine leadership behaviors within executives operating in the non-profit environment, a group that is under-represented in mainstream leadership literature. The researcher concluded, with the endorsement of her chair and committee, which if executed with appropriate diligence and controls, one-on-one interviews would provide valuable qualitative data on the current leadership employed by the highlighted non-profit organizations. The conclusions reached through this process helped to identify opportunities for development that will improve workplace efficiency, improve leadership capabilities and strengthen tenure.

The review of methods and procedures included a detailed description of the subjects in the study, the purposes and methods of the study, and the procedures for the study and an explanation of all instrumentation components. A secondary function was addressed through the presentation of the research design. This discussion also incorporated a review of scope, primary and secondary approaches, and general procedures. In conclusion, *A Qualitative Examination: Ways of Leading Among Non-Profit Executives* explored and served to broaden the existing body of research and knowledge. The 2008 Silver Study extended insight by discerning transferable factors gained from the life experience of the participants. Further, the qualitative research methodology applied in this study demonstrated the viability of the multiple-interview process endorsed by Siedman (1998) as a means for deeply examining the philosophy and actions of seasoned leaders.

REFERENCES

Blanchard, K., & Hodges, P. (2003). *The servant leader: Transforming your heart, head, hands, and habits.* Nashville, TN: J. Countryman/Thomas Nelson.

Bogdan, R. C., & Biklen, S. K. (1998). *Qualitative research for education: An introduction to theory and methods* (3rd ed.). Boston, MA: Allyn & Bacon.

Byrne, M. (2001, February). Sampling for qualitative research. *Association of Operating Room Nurses Journal, 73.*2494–498.

Capra, F. (1996). *The web of life.* New York, NY: Doubleday.

Creswell, J. W. (1994). *Research design: Qualitative and quantitative approaches.* Thousand Oaks, CA: Sage Publications.

Creswell, J. W. (2002). *Educational research: Planning, conducting, and evaluating quantitative and qualitative research.* Upper Saddle River, NJ: Merrill Prentice Hall.

Creswell, J. W. (2003). Research design: Qualitative, quantitative, and mixed methods approaches (2nd ed.). Thousand Oakes, CA: Sage Publications.

Denzin, N. K., & Lincoln, Y. S. (eds.) (2000). *Handbook of quality research* (2nd ed.). Thousand Oaks, CA: Sage Publications.

Dicicco-Bloom, B., & Crabtree, B. F. (2006, April).The qualitative research interview. *Medical Education, 40*(4), 314–321.

Donalek, J. G. (2005). Demystifying nursing research: The interview in qualitative research. *Urologic Nursing. 23*(2), 124–125.

Dym, B., & Hutson, H. (2006). *Leadership in nonprofit organizations: Lessons from the third sector.* Thousand Oaks: CA: Sage Publications.

Farber, N. (2006, June). Conducting qualitative research: A practical guide for school counselors. *Professional School Counseling, 9,* I. 5, 367–375.

Gardner, H. (1983). *Frames of mind: The theory of multiple intelligences* (10th anniversary ed.). New York, NY: Basic Books.

Gardner, H. (1993). *Multiple intelligences.* New York, NY: Basic Books.

Gardner, H. (1995). *Leading minds: An anatomy of leadership.* New York, NY: Basic Books.

Gardner, H. (1999) *Intelligence reframed: Multiple intelligences in the twenty-first century.* New York, NY: Basic Books.

Gardner, H. (2007, March). The ethical mind. *Harvard Business Review,* 51–56.

Greenleaf, R., & Spears, L. (2002). *Servant leadership: A journey into the nature of legitimate power and greatness.* Mahwah, NJ: Paulist Press.

Leedy, P. D., & Ormrod, J. E. (2001). *Practical research: Planning and design* (7th ed.). Upper Saddle River, NJ: Merrill Prentice-Hall.

Makowski, E. S., & Stein, C. H. (2004). Asking, witnessing, interpreting, knowing: Conducting qualitative research in community psychology. *American Journal of Community Psychology, 33,* 21.

Manen, M. (1990). *Researching lived experience: Human science for an action sensitive pedagogy.* Ontario, NY: The State University of New York.

Melanson, J. (2004). Conducting qualitative market research. *LIMRA'S MarketFacts Quarterly, 23,* 3, 26–28.

Meltzoff, J. (1998). *Critical thinking about research: Psychology in related fields.* Washington, DC: American Psychological Association.

Merriam, S. (1998). *Case study research in education: A qualitative approach.* San Francisco, CA: Jossey-Bass.

Millar, B. (1990). Too many charities. *Chronicle of Philanthropy.* 2, 1–19.

Moustakas, C. (1994). *Phenomenological research methods.* Thousand Oaks, CA: Sage Publications.

Neuman, W. L. (2003). *Social research methods* (5th ed.). Upper Saddle River, NJ: Prentice Hall.

Oakley, A. (2004). The researcher's agenda for evidence. *Evaluation and Research in Education, 18.*

Patton, M. Q. (2002). *Qualitative evaluation methods* (10th ed.). Beverly Hills, CA: Sage Publications.

Ponterotto, J. (2005). Qualitative research in counseling psychology: A primer on research paradigms and philosophy of science. *Journal of Counseling Psychology, 52*(2), 126–136.

Pratt, M., & Foreman, P. (2000, January). Classifying managerial responses to multiple organizational identities. *The Academy of Management Review, 25,* 18–42.

Rennie, D. (2002). Qualitative research: History, theory and practice. *Canadian Psychology* special issue, *43*(3).

Rubin, H., & Rubin, I. (1995). *Qualitative interviewing: The art of hearing data.* Thousand Oaks, CA: Sage Publications.

Seidman, I. (1998). *Interviewing as qualitative research*. New York, NY: Teachers College.

Simon, M., & Frances, J.B. (2002). *The dissertation and research cookbook*. Dubuque, IA: Kendall Hunt.

Stemler, S. (2003). An overview of content analysis. Retrieved from http://pareonline.net/getvn.asp?v=7&n=17.

Tierney T. (Producer). (2004). *The emerging leadership crisis in the nonprofit sector* [Video clip]. Bridgespan Group. A Discussion with Tom Tierney May 5, 2004 Stanford Graduate School of Business. Retrieved electronically from http://www.gsb.stanford.edu/pmp/events/2003–2004.html.

Weiss, R. (2004). In their own words: making the most of qualitative interviews. *Contexts, 3*, 4, 44–51. American Sociological Association.

Whitley, R., & Crawford, M. (2005). Qualitative research in psychiatry. *Canadian Journal of Psychiatry, 50*(2), 108–114.

Wilson, T. D. (2002, September 11–13). *Alfred Schutz, phenomenology and research methodology for information behaviour research*. A paper delivered at ISIC4, the Fourth International Conference on Information Seeking in Context, Lusiada University, Lisbon, Portugal.

About the Author

Dr. Gillian Silver is an accomplished integrated marketing communications and strategic planning professional. Her experience spans corporate-level positions for companies with domestic and international operations. She has nearly two decades in the higher education arena preparing Bachelor's, Master's and Doctorate level students. Dr. Gillian's student-oriented philosophy has earned her numerous awards from multiple institutions.

She holds the Accredited Business Communicator designation from IABC, and was named IABC's "Communicator of the Year," and NAWBO's "Woman of the Year/Marketing." Dr. Gillian was twice recognized with the "Women of Excellence/Faculty Award" by the College of Southern Nevada. The institution also selected her for the "President's Service Award," and she received the Mediators of Southern Nevada's "Peacemaker's Award."

Dr. Gillian achieved a Ph.D. in Organizational Leadership from the University of Phoenix, School of Advanced Studies, a Master's in Organizational Development (MS) from the University of Phoenix, and a both a Bachelor's in Mass Communications/Journalism (BS) and a Bachelor's in Fine Arts (BA) from Stephens College.

Published works include her dissertation: *A Qualitative Examination: Ways of Leading Among Non-Profit Executives,* and the book *The Consumer Learner: Emergence and Expectations of a Customer Service Mentality in Post-Secondary Education* with co-author Dr. Cheryl Lentz.

Please contact Dr. Gillian Silver at gsilver@strategicresource.com

PHENOMENOLOGY

CHAPTER 5

Exploring the Experiences of Complementary Nurses: A Qualitative Phenomenology Study

Dr. Susan Kristiniak

The intention of this chapter is to examine the methodology applied in the 2011 Kristiniak Study. The research explored the issues and challenges in healthcare delivery in the early 21st century which impacted the role of nurses in maintaining holistic care modalities and finding satisfaction in their profession (Sharoff, 2008; Ward, 2002). Specifically, the work considers the implications of Baby Boomer nurses who are reaching retirement age, and thereby compounding the nursing shortage in the United States. Patients from the Baby Boomer generation present great demands on healthcare delivery systems through increased patient care needs (Buerhaus, Auerbach, & Staiger, 2009; Carlson, 2009). The combination of variables in healthcare delivery environments warrants evaluations of nursing job satisfaction. Nursing leaders must strategize and identify mechanisms to improve nursing satisfaction. In the era of nursing shortages and an aging nursing workforce, the importance of maintaining nursing satisfaction and retention is critical for nursing leadership (Perry, 2008).

The 2011 Kristiniak Study reflected on inquiries into nursing satisfaction that began in the 1940s and continued through 2009, which concluded staffing levels, shared governance, administrative support, opportunities, benefits, and working conditions are significant elements to satisfaction (Gugerty, 2008; Medical News Today, 2008). Identifying nurses as healers might facilitate patient-nurse connections and yield a strategy to improve nursing satisfaction (Taylor, 2007; Watson, 2009). However, incorporating holistic nursing in an era of technology-focused nursing remains a challenge in the 21st century. It was suggested by the literature that by integrating complementary therapies and providing healing environments, nurses can create a work environment conducive to professional satisfaction (Sharoff, 2008).

The 2011 Kristiniak Study documents how healthcare consumers have begun to recognize the practice of holistic care interventions and the importance of care providers remaining current in such interventions (National Center for Complementary and Alternative Medicine [NCCAM], 2009). Consumers using complementary therapies seek caring experiences and partnerships with healthcare practitioners who view the whole person rather than only the disease. Consumers seeking holistic healing recognize the mind, body, and spirit as important components in maintaining wellness (Bennett, 2009).

NATURE OF THE STUDY

The general problem addressed in the 2011 Kristiniak Study was the nursing workforce instability resulting from (a) the economic downturn, (b) staffing restrictions, (c) reported shortages, and (d) the lack of retention because of dissatisfaction among nurses. The specific problem examined was nurse dissatisfaction based on decreased patient contact. This study addressed the specific problem of nursing satisfaction and the integration of complementary therapies and creation of healing environments.

The 2011 Kristiniak Study involved a qualitative approach to understand the experiences of nurses who integrated complementary therapy care practices into their intervention strategies, and who reconnected with the holistic foundation of nursing care. Qualitative method goes beyond a quantitative approach that could have measured satisfaction with metric measurement to collect nurses' satisfaction. To get to the depth and breadth of the nurses' experiences required an interview process that allowed the participants to describe their stories of patient interactions and experiences. Exploring nurses' perceptions involved further analysis that could probe the interview responses and required being attentive to communication that extends beyond language. Satisfaction in phenomenological design seeks to understand tone, body language, and choice of words as a means of understanding the phenomena.

THEORETICAL FRAMEWORK

The integration of nursing theory and leadership frameworks formed the basis for Kristiniak's qualitative, phenomenological study. While the study found application for healthcare leadership in offering strategies not yet considered for nursing retention, the integration of complementary therapies, enhancing nurses' scope of care delivery was aligned with theoretical application. Watson's (2009) Caring Science provided the fundamental component of healing experiences which represents the foundation of nursing care and the basis for the study approach to reestablishing healing environments. Neuman and Fawcett (2011) defined the individual client (nurse) as the *total person* or *total system*. The Neuman Systems Model included the identification of holistic nursing practices as the simultaneous consideration of all factors that have meaning for wellness in any given clinical situation. The methodology for capturing nurses' perceptions of their experiences was an adaptation of Breckenridge's *Health Care Focus Framework* © (Breckenridge, 1982). Breckenridge developed a schematic presentation that captured patient's perceptions of their selection of care delivery. This model had previously been adapted by Kristiniak, Breckenridge, and Soniak (2011) that identified the return of equilibrium or balance achieved when aromatherapy was used with geriatric, demented patients with agitation. The model's flexibility provides a graphic presentation of a prevention intervention used by the researcher to demonstrate the effects of a strategy to reestablish equilibrium in a system. For the 2011 Kristiniak Study, the equilibrium was defined as nursing satisfaction and the prevention intervention was the integration of complementary therapies into the scope of nursing practice (see Appendix A).

Transformational leadership and the Magnet Recognition Model provided the framework and the underlying theme of leadership support and motivation in 2011 Kristiniak Study (American Nurses Credentialing Center, 2009). Transformational leadership involves the ability to motivate others to pursue high expectations of the leaders' vision. The concentration is placed on maintaining a vision, mission, and positive image in the minds of followers and other leaders. Such leaders emphasize values, ethics, standards, and long-term goals. This form of leader maintains hope and inspiration by sharing in the investment of the vision (Yoder-Wise, 2010). The foundation of transformational leadership in the Magnet Model supports the empowerment of nurses to expand the scope of care and select caring interventions. The leaders within the healthcare delivery system promote challenging and educational opportunities (e.g., training programs and resources) to integrate such practices. Leadership's ability to embrace innovative strategies subsequently empowers the nurses who provide direct care. Maintaining equilibrium is possible when nurses (a) find satisfaction with care delivery, (b) enhance quality, and (c) sustain a wellness-focused healing environment (Aiken, 2005; Watson, 2007).

RESEARCH DESIGN

The qualitative approach provided an effective means for examining the study phenomenon (i.e., nurses' experiences using complementary therapies) and obtaining a richer account of the 2011 Kristiniak Study population's experiences. The foundations of hermeneutical phenomenology were rooted in the works of van Manen (1990) and Heidegger (1962). The German philosopher, Husserl (1859–1939), first presented phenomenology, and Heidegger (1889–1976) explored and expanded the theory. Phenomenology is a human science based in the human world of lived experiences (Moustakas, 1994; van Manen, 1990). Hermeneutics (i.e., hermeneutical phenomenology) pertains to the achievement of meaning in everyday, lived experiences. Van Manen proposed that lived experiences register only in the realm of consciousness. Reflective review of lived experiences becomes a retrospective rather than introspective analysis because the review occurs at a time different from the actual experience. The participating nurses provided the researcher with descriptions of their experiences. These expressions thus created an understanding of their healing environments and use of complementary therapies. The qualitative method applied in the 2011 Kristiniak Study did not involve summarizing the responses from the participants but included analyzing, describing, interpreting, and determining constructs (Moustakas, 1994).

For the 2011 Kristiniak Study, a Complementary Nurses' Perception Interview Guide was developed by the researcher that provided semi-structured, open-ended questions to explore the experiences of complementary nurses. Prior to initiation of the study, the guide was pilot tested for face validity with a purposeful sample of five nurses. The use of a face-to-face interview guide allowed the researcher to go beyond the language of the responses to gain the depth and breadth of the complementary nurses' experiences. The interview process was consistent with the participants' abilities to make meaning of experiences through language and affirmed the importance of their stories. The goal of the interview process was to have nurses tell their stories of holistic caring, expressing personal and accurate experiences pertinent to the study topic. Using the Complementary Nurses' Perception Interview Guide approach for naturalistic inquiry enables the participants to elaborate on information in response to the guided questions (Breckenridge, 2002; Fawcett, 1999).

APPROPRIATENESS OF THE DESIGN

Phenomenological research is appropriate for nursing studies because the focus of phenomenological studies involves understanding the experiences of others and meeting a person's needs in a holistic manner (Polit & Beck, 2010). Heidegger (1962) focused on uncovering hidden phenomena and the importance of the participants' concepts. Attention to tone, choice of language, and emotions added to the discussion and were considered by the researcher to be important in hermeneutical phenomenology. Van Manen's (1990) approach included elements to increase thoughtfulness and ability to capture the experiences.

Hermeneutical phenomenology was the best method for understanding the nurses' lived experiences based on their interpretations. Phenomenologists' belief that understanding comes from lived experiences required the researcher to become part of the experience, participating in the discussions to gain insight of the experiences. These experiences cannot be measured or weighed as they can go beyond the conscious level (Moustakas, 1994). The researcher who must have meaningful understanding of the phenomenon to participate in this exploration must also be aware of his/her own biases and remain objective in the exploration. The use of a Complementary Nurses' Perception Interview Guide by Kristiniak (2011) prompted meaningful inquiry based on the understanding of the phenomenon while providing a consistent approach to uncovering the participants' descriptions. The analysis of the interviews required the researcher's understanding, recognizing the need to bracket biases and beliefs that permitted an openness to explore the new experiences. The 2011 Kristiniak Study required the researcher, a complementary nursing leader at the study site, to consciously approach this method selection and the challenges to collect meaningful understanding from the participants when they were interviewed.

RESEARCH QUESTION

The significance of the 2011 Kristiniak Study is the exploration of an opportunity for nurses to participate in providing healing environments through complementary care interventions and healthcare leaders to improve retention and satisfaction among members of the largest workforce in healthcare (i.e., nurses). The instability of the nursing workforce and the increase in consumer healthcare demand contribute to the importance of satisfying and retaining qualified nurses (Rosseter, 2008; U.S. Census Bureau, 2006). These considerations prompted the researcher to ask the following questions:

1. How do nurses who use complementary therapies perceive their nursing care delivery?

2. How do nurses who use complementary therapies perceive their professional satisfaction?

The research questions guided the identification of nurses' perceptions about integrating complementary therapies and how such therapies contributed to holistic care opportunities and perceived satisfaction in their profession.

POPULATION

The population was a purposeful sample of registered nurses from one place of employment (i.e., the study site). The study site was a mid-Atlantic community, teaching hospital in Abington, Pennsylvania. The site was appropriate for the research because of the hospital's reputation for transforming nursing practice to include complementary therapies in educational programs for bedside nursing care delivery. Innovation of nursing care delivery at the study site reflected the Magnet Model of nursing care and the transformational approach by nursing leadership at the site. The hospital's adaptation of integrating complementary therapy at the acute care level placed this site in the small category of hospitals (37%) across the country recognizing this type of nursing care (American Hospital Association 2009). Nurses eligible for participation in the study had completed education and were deemed competent to practice identified complementary therapies as part of their nursing care.

DATA COLLECTION

The pilot test to determine the Complementary Nurses' Perception Interview Guide use was conducted with five participants. The purpose was to determine the clarity and appropriateness of the interview questions for use in the final study. Each participant took part in individual, face-to-face interviews during which they responded to the questions. Audio digital recording of the interviews enabled review of the participants' responses. The pilot study participants had the additional role of indicating whether the interview questions were clear, promoted discussion, and pertained to the study purpose. The pilot test afforded the researcher an opportunity to put into practice the Complementary Nurses' Perception Interview Guide while allowing for a critique of content, flow of the questions, and the language of each of the questions.

Data collection involved recording the nurses' responses to six open-ended interview questions and probe questions. Hermeneutical analysis in the Heideggerian tradition of interactive and simultaneous interpretive inquiry took place with the goal of understanding nurses' experiences using complementary therapies (Moustakas, 1994). The interview questions included the following:

1. Describe your current complementary therapy nursing practice.

2. Describe your personal decision-making that prompted your use of complementary modalities.

3. Describe how using complementary therapies contribute to your experience of providing healing environments for your patients.

4. How is the use of complementary therapies recognized in your practice, by patients, families, and peers?

5. Describe how the use of complementary modalities presented any challenges or rewards.

   Probe questions:

   a. Describe how you found time available to create a healing experience.

   b. Describe how patients, family members, and caregivers were either accepting of complementary therapies or resistant to the intervention.

   c. Describe any opportunities you experienced to educate patients, and family members, and caregivers in complementary therapies.

6. Describe your personal response after using a complementary therapy intervention in your nursing practice.

A purposeful sample of 16 participants completed face-to-face private interviews, which were tape recorded, and transcribed to allow for the researcher's review. Each interview was compared against the tape recorded data and again following the transcription. Each participant reviewed the transcribed, typed text for validation of the content of responses to provide triangulation.

DATA ANALYSIS

The pilot test participants indicated that the interview questions prompted responses about (a) their use of complementary therapies from a clinical perspective, and (b) their self-reflection on their experiences providing such therapies. The participants all agreed that the Complementary Nurses' Perception Interview Guide questions prompted discussion, and the participants did not recommend changing the wording for any of the questions.

The Complementary Nurses' Perception Interview Guide was determined as a reliable tool to conduct the study. The tool's questions rely on the perceptions of the experiences of the participants. Perception is the foundation of knowledge in phenomenological studies. Identification of a phenomenon occurs through (a) grouping experiences, (b) validating the information, and (c) creating new meanings in the experiences (Moustakas, 1994). Data analysis in qualitative research involves three major components. Synthesizing (i.e., sifting the data) involves determining typical occurrences and variations of the phenomenon and study participants. Comprehension is the understanding of the data collected. Theorizing is a systematic sorting that reveals alternative explanations of the phenomenon. Recontextualizing involves the development of a theory that is generalizable to other groups with the same characteristics (Polit & Beck, 2010).

DATA CODING

Qualitative research data analysis has historically been tedious with manual reviews of lengthy interview or observational data that was coded to identify theme emergence. Technology has provided software data analysis to identify keyword frequencies and prevalence. The 2011 Kristiniak Study used NVivo8 qualitative software by QSR International to extrapolate word frequencies and theme occurrences. The NVivo8 system provided a sophisticated workspace to classify, sort, and arrange information (QSR International, 2010).

The determination of sample size in qualitative research is derived by achieving theoretical saturation. The 2011 Kristiniak Study identified 30 participants in the study proposal. According to Polit and Beck (2010), qualitative research involves the study of a few individuals or cases to elicit in-depth information about the individuals' experiences. Data saturation occurs at the point when no new information emerges and additional information would be redundant.

Theoretical saturation was established when the first 13 participants interviews were reviewed with NVivo8 system and word frequency prevalence was identified. An additional three interviews were conducted and word frequency prevalence confirmed saturation of the collected data.

THEME EMERSION

The review of keyword frequencies that emerged from the analysis of the interview responses led to the identification of themes in the current study. The NVivo8 software facilitated the development of nodes (i.e., coding categories for analyzing data). Tree nodes emerged from the data, and many of the tree nodes had *child nodes* or subcategories that created variability in the emerging categories. Four major themes were identified in this study. The individual themes that emerged from the participants' narratives were then analyzed, deconstructed, and related to the current literature. Further exploration of the transcribed text and recognition of the participants' emotions helped to determine the intention and meaning behind the participants' stories. Categorization, synthesis, and reconstruction of the participants' rich descriptions ultimately led to a deep understanding of the study phenomenon.

Theme 1: Complementary therapies. All participants described their use of complementary therapies in narratives of patient care. The stories conveyed many feelings and captured the passion and energy of the integration of complementary practices. The participants acknowledged the dedication of leaders at the study site as supportive of the complementary scope of nursing practice. The nurses mentioned the availability of education in the modalities and established standards of practice, consistent with the identified values of complementary nurses (Sharoff, 2008; Wallis, Peerson, Young, Parkinson, & Grant, 2004; Yom & Lee, 2008). Sub themes of decision making and stakeholder recognition were identified, and served to capture the participants' autonomy in patient care delivery. Decision making further identified the concept of holism in practice versus need-based care delivery. The integration of complementary nursing care was described in relation to patient and family, physician, and peer perceptions.

Theme 2: Healing. The concept of healing that encompasses care that may not offer curative outcomes aligns with the philosophy of CAM therapies (Antigoni & Dimitrios, 2009). All participants described healing using language that identified presence, non-curative, and curative interventions. Other healing environments were described with attention to the physical space of the patient consistent with caring described by Nightingale (1969).

The sub theme of caring presence emerged not only in the language of the interviews but in the emotion and energy of the participants. The storytelling of patient interventions and patients' responses elicited strong emotions and increase in the volume and tone of the participants during their disclosures. Consistent with previous researchers who aligned compassionate care with the integration of CAM therapies, the participants in the 2011 Kristiniak Study shared these emotional experiences (Shanahan, 2006).

Theme 3: Nurses' feelings. Nurses frequently reported the feelings associated with their experiences of integrating CAM therapies into their scope of nursing practice. The nurses' feelings were positive and negative emotional responses to their added scope of practice, their patients' responses, and some negative perceptions. The theoretical frameworks described by Neuman and Fawcett (2011) and Watson (2009) include nurses' emotional responses. Nurses' perceptions of their emotions were prevalent in the interviews and described in 35 separate references by the 16 participants. Watson's transpersonal caring embodies the shared experiences of nurses and their patients when implementing care. The concept of intentionality incorporates a sense of mindfulness that guides behavior and creates the concept of *being*, not simply *doing* in providing nursing care (Watson, 2009).

Neuman's Systems Model is based on recognition of the environment as it contributes to interpersonal, intrapersonal, and extrapersonal stressors that create imbalance. Breckenridge's (2011) adaptation of Neuman's concepts incorporated a prevention intervention model with variables that can influence stability. The model allowed interventions to be introduced at the primary, secondary, or tertiary levels. The use of complementary therapies added a secondary intervention, with the identification of workforce instability, in hopes of impacting nursing satisfaction. Positive and negative feeling identification helped explore the full scope of the secondary intervention.

The sub theme of positive feelings occurred in three primary areas of increased scope of practice, professional identification, and sense of fulfillment. The sub theme of negative feelings occurred in four references. Comments about feelings helped the researcher to explore all aspects of the challenges as perceived by the participants. Negative feelings were tied to the component of time as it pertained to availability to provide a CAM therapy, or use a particular CAM therapy. Feelings of inadequacy occurred when time constraints prevented the use of CAM therapy. Time was identified as a separate theme to further explore the impact of time in the participant's experiences.

Theme 4: Time. The most frequent challenge for the participants was time. The emphasis on time as a challenge to providing complementary care was unexpected. Time is a critical factor in bedside nurses' coordination and prioritization of patient care. Antigoni and Dimitrios (2009) identified workloads and staffing ratios as inhibiting CAM practices. Not all participants mentioned time as an inhibitory factor to integrating CAM therapies. Some of the participants could prioritize CAM modalities and integrate complementary practices into care without failing in their personal performance expectations. Two sub themes (i.e., challenges and opportunities) emerged from the major theme of time.

A total of 56% of the participants who embraced the concept of holistic nursing practice recognized time issues, but the participants had redefined their nursing practice to include the CAM interventions in their daily care delivery. The participants attributed some of their success in integrating CAM therapies to the supportive organizational culture of the study site. Integrating CAM therapies in the traditional scope of nursing practice enabled the study participants to develop satisfaction in their care practices and professional identification. The 2011 Kristiniak Study results indicate opportunities for healthcare leaders who seek to improve nursing satisfaction and workforce stability.

INFERENCES FROM THE STUDY

The 2011 Kristiniak Study was an exploration of nurses' experiences to determine whether the inclusion of complementary care practices in their scope of care impacted the nurses' overall satisfaction. A relationship exists between nursing satisfaction and the variables of quality care and retention (Aiken, Clarke, & Sloane, 2002; Aiken, 2005; Buerhaus, Donelan, Ulrich, & Norman, 2005a, 2005b; Gould, Drey, & Berridge, 2007; Shanahan, 2006). Leaders at the study site had developed a shared governance approach to facilitate nurse participation in decision making within the nursing department, and the result was support for the integration of CAM therapies in nurses' practice. The development of the Integrative Nursing Council reflected the Magnet designation of the study site. The Integrative Nursing Council was a cohort of like-minded nurses who promoted common goals of CAM therapy and holistic care practices throughout the organization. Nursing leaders' approval of the council fostered the nurses' sense of recognition.

Transformational leaders optimize team performance and promote hope with purpose and direction (Yukl, 2006). The creation of opportunities, achievement of objectives, and delivery of objectives can result in high quality care for patients and fulfill healthcare organizational missions and visions (Yoder-Wise, 2010). Based on the national economic downturn, leaders at the study site imposed a reduction of workforce that included nursing staff during the data collection period. The 2011 Kristiniak Study revealed that leaders maintained nurse-patient ratios, but the event likely added to the (a) strain on the remaining nurses, (b) nurse dissatisfaction, and (c) organizational instability. The shift in organizational structure might have impacted the participants' feelings about integrating CAM therapies.

Nurse and healthcare leaders have recognized the importance of nurse satisfaction in healthcare delivery (Aiken, 2005; Aiken et al.,

2002). Nursing satisfaction and alignment between recruitment and retention efforts contribute to the stability of the nursing workforce (Carlson, 2009). The inclusion of CAM therapies in nursing care enabled the participants to (a) advance their professional development, (b) become empowered with autonomous nursing care interventions, and (c) become fulfilled in their interactions with patients. Watson (2007) and Nightingale (1969) described the importance of maintaining a focus on nursing care and the participants in the current study identified such a focus as contributing to their professional identification and satisfaction. The study findings include nurses' positive perceptions that reduce the risk of imbalance and instability in the context of job satisfaction.

The risks of time constraints and changing healthcare delivery expectations might necessitate a concentrated effort. Leadership's role to ensure inclusion of CAM concepts and practices as core components of nursing practice might require additional consideration. The 2011 Kristiniak Study results indicate a relationship between (a) nurses' inclusion of complementary therapies in their scope of practice and (b) nurses' perception of fulfillment, job satisfaction, and professional identification.

RECOMMENDATIONS FOR FUTURE RESEARCH

Diverse opportunities exist for further studies pertaining to CAM therapies, nurses, patients, and healthcare leadership. Studies of CAM therapies began in the late 20th century. The National Center for Complementary and Alternative Medicine (NCCAM) promotes and supports research to determine the efficacy and outcomes of CAM interventions. Leaders at the study site supported specific CAM modalities (i.e., aromatherapy, guided imagery, and Reiki), and further studies of such modalities might have a focus on patient-care outcomes or nurses' self-care practices.

The participants in the 2011 Kristiniak Study frequently mentioned time in their interview responses. Some nurses were able to prioritize complementary therapy integration, and others used decision making reflective of traditional medical practice, matching interventions with symptoms. Further studies might involve exploring nurses' ability to adapt holistic caring experiences, and the role of holistic practice, aside from complementary care interventions, in improving nursing satisfaction.

The 2011 Kristiniak Study explored nurses' perceptions of their use of complementary therapy in their practice. This approach to collecting participants' (nurses') stories captured the essence of their experiences and revealed key findings that demonstrated the intervention of complementary therapy integration as contributing to nursing satisfaction. The use of phenomenology design allowed for Kristiniak to explore the feelings and passion of the participants through their use of language and their presence in the interview process. The process of ongoing data analysis integrated the researcher as a component to the process with the expectation of reflection and not simply a reviewer of collected data. Qualitative research with phenomenology design selection aligned with the study's approach to capture the participant's discussions in the depth of the descriptions of patient care experiences and professional identification that revealed their professional satisfaction.

REFERENCES

Aiken, L. (2005). Improving patient safety: The link between nursing and quality of care. *Research in Profiles, 12.* Retrieved from http://www.investigatorawards.org/downloads/research_in_profiles_iss12_feb2005.pdf

Aiken, L., Clarke, S., & Sloane, D. (2002). Hospital nursing staffing and patient mortality, nurse burnout and nursing satisfaction. *Journal of American Medical Association, 288*(16), 1987–1993. doi: 10.1001/jama.288.16.1987

American Hospital Association. (2009). *Use of CAM at hospitals continues increase, driven by patient demand.* Washington, DC. Retrieved from http://www.tcmstudent.com/main/Use%20of%20CAM%20at%20at Hospitals%20Continues%20Increase%20Driven%20by%20Patient%20Demand.html

American Nurses Credentialing Center (2009). *Magnet recognition program overview.* Silver Spring, MD. Retrieved from http://nursecredentialing.org/Magnet/ProgramOverview.aspx

Antigoni, F., & Dimitrios, T. (2009). Nurses' attitudes towards complementary therapies. *Health Science Journal, 3*(3), 149–157. Retrieved from http://www.hsj.gr/volume3/issue3/334.pdf

Bennett, D. (2009). Holistic therapies: How nurses can learn complementary and alternative medicine. *RN,* 38–41. Retrieved from http://www.modernmedicine.com/modernmedicine/Modern+Medicine+Now/Holistic-therapies-How-nurses-can-learn-complement/ArticleStandard/Article/detail/584999

Breckenridge, D. M. (1982). Adaptation of the Neuman Systems Model for renal clients. In B. Neuman, *The Neuman Systems Model. Application to nursing education and practice.* Norwalk, CT: Appleton-Century-Crofts.

Breckenridge, D. M. (1995). Nephrology practice and directions for nursing research. In B. Neuman, *The Neuman systems model* (3th ed., pp. 499–507). Norwalk, CT: Appleton-Century-Crofts.

Breckenridge, D. M. (2002). Using the Neuman Systems Model to Guide Nursing Research in the United States. In B. Neuman & J. Fawcett (Eds.), *The Neuman systems model* (4th ed., pp. 176–182). Upper Saddle River, NJ: Pearson Education.

Breckenridge, D. M. (2011). The Neuman Systems Model and evidence-based nursing practice. In B. Neuman & J. Fawcett (Eds.), *The Neuman Systems Model* (5th ed., pp. 245–251). Upper Saddle River, NJ: Pearson Education.

Buerhaus, P., Auerbach, D., & Staiger, D. (2009). The recent surge of nurse employment: Causes and implications. *Health Affairs, 28*(4), 657–658. Retrieved from http://content.healthaffairs.org/cgi/content/abstract/28/4/w657

Buerhaus, P., Donelan, K., Ulrich, B., & Norman, L. (2005a). Hospital RNs' and CNOs' perceptions of the impact of the nursing shortage on the quality of care. *Nursing Economics, 23*(5), 214–221. Retrieved from www.medscape.com/viewarticle/515430_5perceptions

Buerhaus, P., Donelan, K., Ulrich, B., & Norman, L. (2005b). Is the shortage of hospital registered nurses getting better or worse? Findings from two recent national surveys of RNs. *Nursing Economics, 23*(2), 61–71. Retrieved from www.content.healthaffairs.org/content/26/1/178.full

Carlson, J. (2009). Nursing shortage eases . . . but only while the recession lasts, experts warn. *Modern Healthcare, 39*(20), 8. Retrieved from www.ncbi.nlm.nih.gov/pubmed/19504695

Fawcett, J. (1999). *The relationship of theory and research* (3rd ed.). Philadelphia, PA: FA Davis.

Gould, D., Drey, N., & Berridge, E. (2007). Nurses' experience of continuing professional development. *Nurse Education Today, 27*(1), 602–609. Retrieved from https://findarticles.com/p/articles/mi_m0748/is_8_19/ai.../pg_7/

Gugerty, L. (2008). Nursing care: A lost art. *Nursing Forum, 43*(3), 160–161. Retrieved from http://www.ncbi.nlm.nih.gov/pubmed/18715349

Heidegger, M. (1962). *Being and time.* London, UK: SCM Press.

Husserl, E. (1987). *Edmund Husserl's phenomenology: A critical commentary.* Bloomington, IN: Indiana University Press.

Kristiniak, S. (2011). *Exploring the experiences of complementary nurses: A qualitative phenomenological study.* Unpublished doctoral dissertation, University of Phoenix.

Kristiniak, S., Breckenridge, D., & Soniak, S. (2010). Effect of lavender aromatherapy on the agitation of patients with dementia in an acute psychiatric setting: A pilot study. Submitted for publication.

Medical News Today. (2008). *Nurse staffing impact quality of patient care.* Retrieved from http://www.medicalnewstoday.com/articles/108796.php

Moustakas, C. E. (1994). *Phenomenological research methods.* Thousand Oaks, CA: Sage Publications.

National Center for Complementary and Alternative Medicine. (2009). *The use of complementary and alternative therapies in the United States.* Retrieved from http://nccam.nih.gov/news/camstats/2007/camsurvey_fs1.htm

Neuman, B., & Fawcett, J. (Eds.). (2011). *The Neuman systems model* (5th ed.). Upper Saddle River, NJ: Pearson Education.

Nightingale, F. (1969). *Notes on nursing: What it is and what it is not.* New York, NY: Dover.

Perry, B. (2008). Shine on: Achieving career satisfaction as a registered nurse. *The Journal of Continuing Education in Nursing, 39*(1), 17–25. Retrieved from www.ncbi.nlm.nih.gov/pubmed?term=Perry+Beth%5Bau%5D

Polit, D., & Beck, C. (2010). *Essentials of nursing research* (7th ed.). Philadelphia, PA: Lippincott, Williams & Wilkins.

Rosseter, R. (2008). Nursing shortage fact sheet. *American Association of Colleges of Nursing.* Retrieved from http://www.aacn.nche.edu/media/pdf/NrsgShortageFS.pdf

QSR International. (2010). *What is qualitative research?* Cambridge, MA. Retrieved from http://www.qsrinternational.com/what-is-qualitative-research.aspx

Shanahan, M. (2006). Integrative care in hospital settings. *American Holistic Nurses Association (AHNA)/American Holistic Medical Association (AHMA) Annual Conference.* Retrieved from www.medscape.com/viewarticle/542205

Sharoff, L. (2008). Holistic nursing and medical-surgical nursing: A natural integration. *Medsurg Nursing, 17*(3), 206–208. Retrieved from http://www.ncbi.nlm.nih.gov/pubmed/18686428

Taylor, H. (2007). Nurse satisfaction: The real key. *Healthcare Financial Management, 61*(2), 22. Retrieved from http://www.allbusiness.com/company-activities-management/operations-customer/10589173–1.html

Van Manen, M. (1990). *Researching lived experience: Human science for an action sensitive pedagogy.* New York, NY: State University of New York Press.

Wallis, M., Peerson, A., Young, J., Parkinson, S., & Grant, S. (2004). Nurses' utilization of complementary therapies: A pilot study exploring scope of practice. *Collegian, 11*(4), 19–25. Retrieved from http://espace.library.uq.edu.au/view/UQ:160497

Ward, S. (2002). Balancing high-tech nursing with holistic healing. *Journal for Specialist in Pediatric Nursing, 7*(2), 81–83. doi: 10.1111/j.1744

Watson, J. (2007). Dr. Jean Watson's human caring theory. *Inova Health.* Retrieved from www.watsoncaringscience.org/caring_science/10caritas.html

Watson, J. (2009). Caring science and human caring theory: Transforming personal and professional practices of nursing and healthcare. *Journal of Health and Human Services, 31*(4), 466–482. Retrieved from http://www.ncbi.nlm.nih.gov/pubmed?term=Watson+Jean%5Bau%5D

Yoder-Wise, P. (2010). *Leading and managing in nursing* (4th ed.). St Louis, MO: Mosby.

Yom, Y., & Lee, K. E. (2008). A comparison of the knowledge of, experience with, and attitudes towards complementary and alternative medicine between nurses and patients in Korea. *Journal of Clinical Nursing, 17*(19), 2565–2572. doi: 10.1111/j.1365–2702.2007.02065.x

Yukl, G. (2006). *Leadership in organizations.* Upper Saddle River, NJ: Prentice Hall.

Appendix A:
Perceived Complementary Nursing Satisfaction

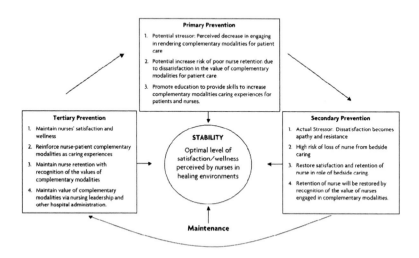

(adapted from Health Care Focus © Breckenridge in Neuman, 1982; 1995; Breckenridge in Neuman & Fawcett, 2011).

About the Author

Dr. Susan Kristiniak holds several accredited degrees, a Bachelors of Science degree in Nursing (BSN) from Gwynedd Mercy College; a Masters of Science in Nursing (MSN) in Integrative Health from University of Phoenix, and a Doctorate in Healthcare Administration (DHA) from University of Phoenix School for Advanced Studies. She holds clinical practice certifications in aromatherapy and is a Reiki Master practitioner and co-chairs the Integrative Nursing Council.

Dr. Susan is a nursing leader in a Philadelphia suburban, community, teaching hospital, Abington Memorial Hospital where she manages a palliative care program and the pastoral care department. She has developed educational programming in Integrative Nursing Care and pain management across the healthcare system. She has conducted multiple research studies using integrative nursing practices. Dr. Susan has presented at both national and international conferences in the area of Integrative nursing practices.

Dr. Susan is certified as an Advanced Holistic Nurse by the American Holistic Nurses Certification Corporation (AHNCC).

Dr. Susan has over 30 years of nursing practice spanning direct patient care to nursing leadership. She has focused on her passion of the integration of holistic nursing care and self care practices.

Dr. Susan Kristiniak can be reached at skristiniak@comcast.net

Motivation and Creativity's Role in Small Business E-Entrepreneurship Innovations

Dr. Nate P. Boyer

This article examines study findings from the 2011 Boyer Study. The qualitative phenomenological examination described how motivation and creativity influences small-business E-entrepreneurs' innovations. According to Gruber and Henkel (2004), E-Entrepreneurship is the "discovery and exploitation of business opportunities in the internet economy" (p. 356). Contemporary media and publications have written much about mid-sized E-entrepreneurial ventures as well as larger E-entrepreneurial ventures such as FaceBook, Google, and Twitter as they have evolved into major businesses. However, there has been a scarcity of scholarly research published on E-entrepreneurial entities when they are in the very early start-up stage. The 2011 Boyer Study population characteristics included E-entrepreneurs (Internet-based sole proprietors, owners, co-founders, presidents, and CEOs). Participants had annual revenues of less than $1 million, were operating for less than 5 years, had fewer than 10 employees, owned service oriented businesses, and were located in Syracuse, NY. The 2011 Boyer Study attempts to address the lack of literature available on small-business, early stage, E-entrepreneurial ventures.

The 2011 Boyer Study used a modified Van Kaam phenomenological method by Moustakas (1994) to present a rare look into the roles motivation and creativity played in the success of 17 E-entrepreneurs. This article provides doctoral learners, researchers, and business analysts with an understanding of how early start-up E-entrepreneurs applied their personal motivation and creativity to generate innovations for their businesses. A critical incident technique interview (CIT) approach, along with semi-structured open-ended questions, was incorporated into the 2011 Boyer Study to assist participants' as they shared the processes they used to generate innovations. CIT interviewing describes incidents over time, where interviewees perceive or remember significant events and retell these experiences as stories (Fillis, 2006). The focus of the 2011 Boyer study was understanding motivation and creativity processes influence on E-entrepreneurs' ability to produce innovations. Research variables included the themes motivation, creativity, E-entrepreneurship, transformational leadership, innovation, social media and social networking (see Table 1).

Research from psychology, organizational behavior, and sociology disciplines were used to support findings. Entrepreneurial motivation (McMullen & Shepherd, 2006), Wallas' creative process (Bernardin & Kemp-Robertso, 2008), and Altshuller's systematic theory of inventive problem solving (TRIZ) ;(Nissing, 2007) were used to help understand motivational and creativity study themes. The knowledge spillover theory of entrepreneurship (Acs, Braunerhjelm, Audretsch, & Carlsson, 2009) and transformational leadership theories (Walumbwa, Avolio, & Zhu, 2008) were also used to assist in understanding themes. The knowledge spillover theory of entrepreneurship suggests that often entrepreneurial innovations are generated inside existing organizations first before they are actually commercialized by entrepreneurs outside of the original organization. Bass' (1985) original model of transformational leadership suggests organic, challenging, and rapidly changing environments are more conducive to the emergence of transformational leaders (Walumbwa, Avolio, & Zhu, 2008). The theories were selected to substantiate the 2011 Boyer Study because of their ability to help explain the most important innovation processes and experiences.

Although the U.S. maintains leadership roles in many aspects of innovation, recent statistics from the Information Technology and Innovation Foundation indicate the lead is decreasing (Atkinson, 2009). Whereas large businesses have financial strength to consistently invest in the innovation process, small businesses may lack the same capacity. Without new mechanisms to help small-businesses generate more innovations, increasing numbers of future inventions will likely come from other nations.

TABLE 1. *2011 BOYER STUDY: SUMMARY OF CORE THEMES*

Theme	Brief Description
Motivation	Entrepreneurial desire to exert effort based on task enjoyment and desire to expend effort for outcomes separate from the task such as recognition or reward. A personal desire to create new unique products/services useful to customers that are profitable, competitive, and available via the Internet.
Creativity	The business process, outcome, and new idea creation component of innovation resulting in product or service differentiation. Generating novel and useful ideas using the Internet. Creativity means creating original ideas, online experiences, products, services, and processes. Possessing an ability to see ordinary things differently.
E-entrepreneurship	Multiple persons are able to interact across local, regional, national, and global geographic and time zones as a user, developer, buyer, and seller. Acquiring, copying, storing, and distributing information electronically may be costly or costless. Globally dispersed users may contribute to innovations through their time and effort freely or for pay and software may be accessible instantaneously. May sell products, services, or both.
Innovation	Ongoing attempt to create something new while at the same time learning, searching and exploring uniquely helpful possibilities for potential customers. A new solution to an old problem that offers a new product, service, process, or combination that also involves use of the Internet.

Transformational leadership	Must have a vision and be able to persuade others to adopt that vision. Leadership behavior must be capable of transforming norms and values of employees to perform beyond their own expectations enabling "open-mindedness and participation"
Social networking	The ability of all interested parties to build and use networks or coalitions with groups and individuals they care about using the Internet. Describes systems that enable users of web sites to acquire knowledge about other users or members abilities, experiences, likes, or dislikes. Social networking identifies, builds, and maintains relationships online.
Social media	Social media are Internet-based tools such as websites, applications and are involved in exchanging user generated communications and content

Creating new innovations and entrepreneurial start-up activities is critical to economic sustainability and global competitiveness (McGibbon & Moutray, 2009). Literature from academia, business, and government organizations identifies small businesses as economic engines representing more than 95% of all businesses and 50% of gross domestic product (Howard, 2006; U.S. Small Business Administration Office of Advocacy, 2009). Despite America's lead in many sectors, India and China graduate 10 times as many engineers and scientists (Wadhwa, Gereffi, Rissing, & Ong, 2007). According to the World Economic Forum, the U.S. ranked second behind Switzerland for global competitiveness (Schwab, 2009). One anticipated research outcome is helping readers understand ways in which the revealed themes potentially influence economic progress. Several positive outcomes might include improving small-business problem-solving processes, leadership training, and organizational success modeling. Another research outcome that could benefit researchers is a better understanding of the increasingly important role social media and social networking play in the success of E-entrepreneurial businesses.

BACKGROUND

The fourth quarter of 2008, marked the worst financial crisis since the 1930s and resulted in the Dow Jones Industrial Average losing more than 20%, and individual investors of publicly traded stocks losing trillions of dollars in stock value (Fisch, 2009). A growing concern is that the U.S. current economic and technological slide from global dominance may negatively impact the country's ability to generate strategic innovations and thus result in fewer competitive advantages in the future (Popkin & Kobe, 2006). Although it is debatable whether countries are being more innovative than the U.S., what is not debatable is the declining number of engineering doctorates, patents, and scientific articles written in the U.S. relative to major European and Asian nations (Bhide, 2009). If the deficit cannot be significantly reduced, it is possible the U.S. may suffer negative economic, financial, and technological consequences.

Within a few months, the 2008 financial crisis eliminated more than $50 trillion in shareholder wealth (El-Erian, 2009). The 2008 crisis forced many businesses to downsize Research and Development (R&D) departments, cut innovation staff, reduce innovation budgets, and in some instances eliminate innovation-oriented efforts altogether (Spahr, 2009). Gibbert, Hoegl, and Valikangas (2007) noted how businesses that continued to invest in R&D and innovation efforts did better than businesses that eliminated innovation investments. If the U.S. cannot meet these foreign innovation challenges, businesses may continue to fall further behind economically, and technologically, and lose their competitive advantages.

As early as the mid-1990s, there were challenges to and questions about the competitive status of America's innovation leadership role (Powers & Leal, 1994). Simultaneous to the challenges and current crisis, Internet-based strategic innovations have been playing a larger role in an increasingly global business environment. The 2011 Boyer Study intended to demonstrate that understanding how motivation and creativity processes influence strategic ideas may offer new insights on regaining global innovation leadership. Defining motivation, creativity, and innovation theories at the personal level could also be useful in understanding the role E-entrepreneurs play globally.

FOCUS ON DATA ANALYSIS METHODOLOGY

A phenomenological design was selected to explore innovation processes in the lived experiences of E-entrepreneurs in central upstate New York. An unbiased phenomenological approach was helpful in identifying participants lived perceptions through understanding and analysis of data derived from semi-structured interviews. Quantitative and grounded theory designs were not selected as the purpose of the 2011 Boyer Study was not to test theories using participants' experiences. The selected design was chosen to assist the exploration and understanding of processes leading to innovations.

The exploratory, theme-focused, and multi-participant nature of a phenomenological research design made it appropriate to accomplish the goals of this study. All participants were assigned an alphanumeric code to protect their identities and interviews were recorded using a digital audio recorder. Data analysis was conducted using a modified Moustakas (1994) approach that included creating and organizing all files. After each interview was completed, electronically transcribed, and reviewed, transcripts were sent to participants for accuracy verification.

Once accuracy was verified, margin notations were made where appropriate, key statements were highlighted, and initial codes were created that associated with important participant statements. For each interview an attempt was made to describe the meaning of the innovation experience based on transcripts of the interview.

Following completion of the interviews the data were completed, transcribed, reviewed, and described transcripts were classified to list and analyze critical statements of interviewees. NVivo 8 qualitative analysis software was used for its ability to upload transcribed interviews, query, produce charts, compare, contrast, manage, and map a variety of multi-media files (Johnson, Buehring, Cassell, & Symon, 2007). Study results were summarized and presented based on research questions and major themes. The potential for bias was reduced by creating a list of semi-structured interview questions used in collecting participant innovation experiences.

Data collection was confined to participants individually referred to the researcher using a snowball sampling technique. By using a snowball sampling technique the number of E-entrepreneurs that were screened for participation in the 2011 Boyer Study was intentionally limited. This technique also severely limited the frequency of interviews scheduled during the data collection and analysis process. The validity of the member checking strategy may have limited the validity of the study as the interview follow-up telephone calls were made a full three months after the interviews were conducted.

FINDINGS

Seven major themes and multiple patterns materialized horizontally as a result of systematically analyzing the participants' descriptions relevant to each question. The elimination of redundant participant contributions, and subsequent clustering of the invariant constituents of experiences, helped to frame the research further. NVivo software was used to manage data in the analysis phase. NVivo was also used to create sources, nodes, queries, classifications, coding patterns, and revealed a large number of textural themes collected from interviews.

Participants' responses to the 14 open-ended, semi-structured questions offered a number of relevant insights for addressing the research questions. The data showed how the Internet influenced personal and professional motivation processes for generating innovations. Results provide a glimpse of participant approaches to creative problem-solving using NVivo to analyze participant responses and Wallas' (1926) creative model to offer insights into the Internet operating environment's influence on new innovations. The themes and patterns that emerged from study results are based on face-to-face participant experiences of innovation. All of the 2011 Boyer Study findings are based on experiences described by participants, meanings, and essence of the phenomenon (Moustakas, 1994). The 2011 Boyer Study contains a discussion of the seven themes revealed from an analysis of the interview questions and is summarized in Table 1.

Data results revealed that E-entrepreneurs may have more opportunities for understanding the difference between social media and social networking than other entrepreneurs who are not dependent on the Internet for their operations. The data results also suggested that understanding the difference between social media and social networking has the potential to give E-entrepreneurs an advantage over other kinds of entrepreneurs if the knowledge is used correctly. Results indicate the use of social media and social networking has been an important factor in the success of participants' businesses and may continue to be important in the future. Current literature suggested Internet-based social networks are increasingly becoming important business tools (Lazaroiu, 2010). According to Shih (2009), social networking stimulates formation of entrepreneurial networks and improves social connections.

Themes were arranged by number of times a theme was mentioned in participant interviews (see Table 2). Themes were derived from research questions, literature associated with small-business based innovation and social media and social networking themes uncovered in participant interviews. Although collection and analysis processes revealed that participants were unfamiliar with phrase transformational leadership, their descriptions often contained leadership characteristics associated with transformational leadership. Participants had different definitions for the phrases social media and social networking (see Table 1).

TABLE 2. *2011 BOYER STUDY: SUMMARY OF THEME DISTRIBUTION*

Themes	Total times mentioned in interviews
Innovation	305
Creativity	263
Motivation	118
Leadership	117
Social media	93
Internet entrepreneurship	55
Social networking	43

The first theme to emerge from the data analysis was the importance of innovation to the overall success of participants' Internet-based businesses. Sixteen (95%) participants indicated use of well-documented innovation generating techniques such as brainstorming, gap analysis, mind mapping, lateral thinking, and listing. No participants used or were familiar with any of the more systematic innovation generating techniques that included TRIZ, Scamper, PIPS, or synectics. One (12%) participant used an unconventional approach to innovation generation using multiple techniques including mind mapping, journaling, lucid dreaming, and Google search as a brainstorming mechanism. Findings discussed adhere to the open innovation theory posited by Chesbrough (Gassmann, Enkel, & Chesbrough, 2010) and the disruptive innovation theory proposed by Christensen (2006).

A second theme emerging from data analysis was how participants used creative processes to generate ideas and solve problems that eventually led to innovations. Participants indicated their individual creative problem-solving processes were learned by parental guidance, watching others engage in solving problems, academic exposure to problem-solving approaches, and by accident. All participants believed creativity played an important role in their businesses remaining competitive. Effective transformational leaders must have creative skills to consistently generate ideas, make decisions, and solve problems for their followers (Sternberg, 2008). No two participants used the same strategy to generate or verify a creative idea.

The third theme to emerge from analyzing interviews was the significance motivation played in participants' innovation generation process. All of the participants believed producing revenue played at least some role in their motivation to generate an innovation. Revenue generation appeared to be less important for participants who were just starting up versus those who had been in existence for a few years. All participants expressed that freedom to work on something of intense personal interest was the major motivator contributing to the ability to innovate.

Although no participant described themselves as being a transformational leader, all participants identified themselves as possessing at least one transformational leadership characteristics: charisma, inspirational motivation, intellectual stimulation, and individual consideration (Clawson, 2006). Participants described their leadership styles as being democratic, open-minded, empathetic, pragmatic, and visionary leaders with no one dominant style. The common leadership thread was a willingness to be flexible with employees while remaining focused on their vision of the business. Participant data indicated shared values such as academic background, parental upbringing, work experience, and shared social experiences. All participants stated they acted as champions for their business and encouraged behaviors enhancing and rewarding employees' intellectual stimulation, exploratory thinking, and inspirational motivation in the innovation process (Avolio, Rotundo, & Walumbwa, 2009).

Kim, Lee, Lee, and Paik (2010) defined social media as a collection of Internet tools and platforms that can be used to share experiences, ideas, and points of view. Participants thought of social media as a tool and social networking as what one does in an online community. Participants confirmed researchers Jones and Iredale's (2009) assertion that learning occurs through the use of social media by entrepreneurs and all of their stakeholders. Participants appeared to understand their motivation to create useful and unique services was enhanced by implementation of social media. Using social media helped participants gain access to more relevant business information faster than without using social media.

Participants also understood there was a difference between social media (the transmission channel) and social networking (the act of texting or chatting). Participants shared that although they knew a difference in the terms, most people used the terms interchangeably. As the study of social media and social networking becomes more established one might expect the terms may not be used so interchangeably in the future.

A sixth theme emerging from data analysis was participants' perception that the field of Internet entrepreneurship was still new. Skinner (2010) defined Internet entrepreneurship as the utilization of a global network for purposes of acquiring worldwide innovation processes involving knowledge intensive products and services. All participants used words such as "new, change or different" when characterizing what motivated them to become E-entrepreneurs. The same words were used to describe what participants thought about the maturity of the E-entrepreneurship field. Participants used words such as "scarce, little, unavailable" to describe the perceived lack of information available on E-entrepreneurship start-up businesses.

All of the participants stated they used both offline and online social networking as a mechanism to remain competitive and stay in touch with their customers, partners, investors, and other stakeholders. Twitter, FaceBook, and LinkedIn were the social networks discussed most often by participants. The Chamber of Commerce and the Service Corps of Retired Executives were the traditional networks discussed most often by participants.

This section discusses how the findings described relate to the two research questions identified in the 2011 Boyer Study. The section uses Csikszentmihalyi's (1996) flow theory and Graham Wallas' (1926) four stages of creative process to address how motivation and creativity may influence participants' ability to innovate using the Internet. Results presented are based on data analyzed in the 2011 Boyer Study.

How does the Internet operating environment influence the motivation process for generating innovations by E-entrepreneurs in central upstate New York? Csikszentmihalyi (1996) suggested that an individual is most happy and productive when they are in a state of flow. Flow is the experience of being fully involved in an activity where an individual is so immersed in what they are doing they are considered to be in what many call the zone (Vickers, 2010).

Flow theory and research originated from a desire to understand intrinsic motivation (Snyder & Lopez, 2009). Csikszentmihalyi (1996) suggested that one's motivation for being creative results from a system of three different elements. The elements include "a culture that contains symbolic rules, a person who brings novelty into the symbolic domain and a field of experts who recognize and validate the innovation" (Csikszentmihalyi, 1996, p. 6).

According to data from the 2011 Boyer Study, several Internet operating environmental systems influenced participants' motivation processes for generating innovations. The processes included easy online access, systems for online operational efficiency, the ability to sell products and or services on a systematic basis, and easy access to social media and social networking systems. Examples of systems influencing participants' operation of an Internet-based business included access to wireless Internet, high-speed broadband services, mobile wireless, and satellite-based Internet access. Other systems that influenced participants' business operations efficiency approach included online systems such as auto responders (automated e-mail response systems), e-commerce software (online business software), and Internet search analytics tools (systems that collect and aggregate keyword statistics for search engine optimization). Examples Internet-based systems that enable businesses and customers to more easily and creatively sell products and services include automated advertising systems such as Google Adsense, Adwords and automated web visitor statistics such as Google Analytics.

Data results indicated easy global access to the Internet and resulting operational efficiencies may encourage participants to be more highly motivated about their participation in the creativity and innovation processes. Although operating exclusively via the Internet does not guarantee a business will be more efficient, participants believed operating exclusively on the Internet did give them at least some competitive advantages. The 2011 Boyer Study data showed participants appeared highly motivated to find the right mix of product and service offerings as they believed doing so might help them hold the lead in their market for a longer period of time. Data results also suggest there was no difference in participant ages ranges and their business having at least some dependence on the use of social media and social networking.

How does the Internet operating environment influence the Wallas (1926) creative problem-solving steps of preparation, incubation, illumination, and verification in generating innovations for

E-entrepreneurs in central upstate New York? Participants offered a variety of responses to Research Question 2. The following paragraphs describe question results identified in participant interviews.

The preparation stage for creative idea generation can be characterized as preliminary work that focuses an individual's mental efforts to explore dimensions of the problem (Bernardin & Kemp-Robertso, 2008). In the preparation stage an individual starts to define the issue, need, or problem by gathering information (Proctor, 2010). Data results discussed suggested participants believed the Internet was in a constant state of change for which the participants needed to be prepared.

During the incubation stage the problem is considered from other perspectives and then set aside for some period of time (Jones, 2004). Although all participants confirmed they experienced the creative problem-solving incubation stage, data results indicated there was no consensus on the amount of time a problem was set aside.

In the illumination or inspiration stage one achieves or discovers insight and sometimes the *ah-ha* moment (Johnson & Carruthers, 2006). The verification stage requires demonstration and elaboration of whether emerging ideas or solutions can satisfy needs and criteria identified in the preparation stage (Sailer, 2011). Data results indicated that unlike the other three stages of Wallas' (1926) creative solving process; all participants appeared to have slightly different approaches to verifying whether solutions worked for their problem.

RECOMMENDATIONS

The study results present the industry with several new insights that have the potential to stimulate increased survival and profitability rates. Potentially interested U.S. constituents include governments, business associations, E-entrepreneurs, academic and business researchers, politicians, investors, business analysts and economists. The 2011 Boyer Study has potential to provide the U.S. E-entrepreneurial marketplace with a competitive advantage. Results from this study could act as a starting point for understanding how advanced problem-solving techniques are usable by E-entrepreneurs and could be useful in creating and generating new innovations on a larger and more rapid scale. The findings may also open new discussions about using motivation, creativity, and advanced problem-solving tools to generate new innovations faster, less expensively, and most importantly at the individual entrepreneurial level.

Recommendations call for industry leaders to initiate discussions with government, nonprofit, academic, and volunteer organizations in making initial acquisitions of advanced problem-solving tools on behalf of E-entrepreneurs. Supporting organizations could also assist with software licensing management and consider monitoring the success of the businesses. By taking the support approach, E-entrepreneurs could reduce the cost associated with identifying, acquiring, learning, customizing, and implementing advanced problem-solving tools and software. The organizational support approach could be a starting point for reduced failure rates for small businesses in general.

Industry entrepreneurial leaders could also focus on nonprofit support organizations and consider merging some portion of support dollars to acquire, make available software, and train E-entrepreneurs to use advanced problem-solving tools. The benefits of embracing an advanced problem-solving tool strategy include the potential for increased business survival rates, increased profitability, improved productivity, and increased global competitiveness. Industry leaders should note the group of entrepreneurial support organizations would be particularly effective as the nonprofits can receive funding support from a wide range of entities including government agencies, academic institutions, commercial businesses, and even other nonprofits.

The 2011 Boyer Study results suggested industry leaders should consider targeting academic support institutions for the adoption of an advanced problem-solving tools strategy. America's top entrepreneurship schools could provide money, consulting, training, research, and support incentives to E-entrepreneurs and offer business planning support on an ongoing basis. Government and academic institutions may have the greatest potential to influence the adoption of advanced problem-solving tools as these organizations tend to have relationships with virtually all of the constituencies that would interface with E-entrepreneurs. The academic institutions could solicit and receive grants and donations to fund the integration of advanced problem-solving tools into the E-entrepreneurs' business and operational plans.

CONCLUSION

E-entrepreneurs face the same problems other small-businesses do including starting businesses for the wrong reasons, insufficient start-up or continuity capital, poor management skills, a poor website, poor planning, and attempts to expand too quickly. The Internet operating environment is unique in providing Internet-based entrepreneurs with instant global access to potential customers. Instant access can have the positive and negative effect of causing an E-entrepreneur to succeed or fail faster.

Governments may be interested in E-entrepreneurs' ability to generate innovations for the impact it may have on the tax base. Business trade association and chamber of commerce leaders may have an interest in the 2011 Boyer Study for the potential competitive impact Internet-based businesses may have on association member businesses. These same organizations might be interested in E-entrepreneurs' innovations so they could share the business models and processes of successful E-entrepreneurial businesses with their members. Existing and potential E-entrepreneurs could be interested in the new study results to assist them in understanding how other entrepreneurs successfully used motivation and creativity to generate new innovations.

Academic researchers may be interested in the new study results as starting point for theory research as there appears to be a scarcity of scholarly literature on E-entrepreneurs. Investors, venture capitalists, and others with a financial interest in the success of small-businesses could use the information included in the new study to refine the psychological investment profile of a potential entrepreneurial investment. Economists might use the new study as a starting point to for more detailed quantitative studies on E-entrepreneurs' impact on the larger U.S. economy. E-entrepreneurs bring a combination of intellectual, technical, and innovative ideas that may effectively compete against foreign innovations. Many of these same entrepreneurs bring newly acquired thinking skills that include how to prepare, incubate, illuminate, and verify creative solutions to difficult innovation oriented problems.

Based on the findings of 2011 Boyer Study, social media and social networking may play a much greater role in the success or failure of E-entrepreneurs' future than initially thought. Social media and social networking appear to be important factors in the success or failure of participants Internet-based businesses. Although all of the participants expressed their belief social media and networking activities would continue to be important to the future of their businesses, participants must still master basic business operational skills to survive and remain competitive in the future.

REFERENCES

Acs, Z., Braunerhjelm, P., Audretsch, D., & Carlsson, B. (2009). The knowledge spillover theory of entrepreneurship. *Small Business Economics, 32*, 15–30. doi: 10.1007/s11187-008-9157-3

Atkinson, R. (2009). An innovation economics agenda for the Obama administration. *Journal of Technology Transfer, 34*, 440–447. doi: 410.1007/s10961-10009-19106-10966

Avolio, B. J., Rotundo, M., & Walumbwa, F. O. (2009). Early life experiences as determinants of leadership role occupancy: The importance of parental influence and rule breaking behavior. *The Leadership Quarterly, 20*(3), 329–342. doi:310.1016/j.leaqua.2009.1003.1015

Bass, B. M. (1985). *Leadership and performance beyond expectations.* New York, NY: Free Press.

Bassell, K. (2010). Social media and the implications for nursing faculty mentoring: A review of the literature. *Teaching and Learning in Nursing, 5*(4), 143–148. doi: 110.1016/j.teln.2010.1007.1007

Bernardin, T., & Kemp-Robertso, P. (2008). Envisioning the future of advertising creativity research. *Journal of Advertising, 37*(4), 131–149. doi: 110.2753/JOA0091–3367370411

Bhide, A. (2009). Where innovation creates value. *McKinsey Quarterly*(2), 119–125.

Blomstrom, S., Boster, F. J., Levine, K. J., Butler, E. M. J., & Levine, S. L. (2008). The effects of training on brainstorming. *Journal of the Communication, Speech & Theatre Association of North Dakota, 21*, 41–50.

Boyd, D. M., & Ellison, N. B. (2007). Social network sites: Definition, history, and scholarship. *Journal of Computer-Mediated Communication, 13*(1), 210–230. doi:210.1111/j.1083–6101.2007.00393.x

Boyer, N. (2011). *A phenomenological study: How motivation and creativity influence small-business Internet entrepreneurs' innovations.* (Unpublished dissertation). University of Phoenix School of Advanced Studies, Phoenix, AZ.

Christensen, C. M. (2006). The ongoing process of building a theory of disruption 2006. *Journal of Product Innovation Management, 23*(1), 39–55. doi: 10.1111/j.1540–5885.2005.00180.x

Clawson, J.G. (2009). *Level three leadership: Getting below the surface.* (4th ed.). Upper Saddle River, NJ: Pearson Prentice Hall.

Csikszentmihalyi, M. (1996). *Creativity: Flow and the psychology of discovery and invention.* New York, NY: Harper/Collins.

Doz, Y., & Kosonen, M. (2009). Embedding strategic agility: a leadership agenda for accelerating business model renewal. *Long Range Planning,* 42(4), 1–13. doi:10.1016/j.lrp.2009.1007.1006

El-Erian, M. A. (2009). Shrinkage. *Foreign Policy, May/June* (172), 88–88.

Fillis, I. (2006). A biographical approach to researching entrepreneurship in the smaller firm. *Management Decision,* 44(2), 198–212. doi: 110.1108/00251740610650193

Fisch, J. E. (2009). Top cop or regulatory flop? the SEC at 75. *Virginia Law Review, 95,* 785–823. Retrieved from http://papers.ssrn.com/sol783/papers.cfm?abstract_id=1392284##.

Gassmann, O., Enkel, E., & Chesbrough, H. (2010). The future of open innovation. *R&D Management, 40*(3), 213–221. doi: 210.1111/j.1467-9310.2010.00605.x

Gibbert, M., Hoegl, M., & Välikangas, L. (2007). In praise of resource constraints. *MIT Sloan Management Review, 48*(3), 15–17.

Gruber, M., & Henkel, J. (2006). New ventures based on open innovation: An empirical analysis of start-up firms in embedded Linux. *International Journal of Technology Management, 33*(4), 356–372. doi:310.1504/IJTM.2006.009249.

Howard, J. (2006). Small business growth: Development of indicators. *Academy of Entrepreneurship Journal, 12*(1), 73–88.

Johnson, H., & Carruthers, L. (2006). Supporting creative and reflective processes. *International Journal of Human-Computer Studies, 64*(10), 998–1030. doi: 1010.1016/j.ijhcs.2006.1006.1001

Johnson, P., Buehring, A., Cassell, C., & Symon, G. (2007). Defining qualitative management research: an empirical investigation. *Qualitative Research in Organizations and Management: An International Journal, 2*(1), 23–42. doi: 10.1108/17465640710749108

Jones, J. (2004). *The Republic of Creative Thought: How to Incorporate Creativity in Your Work and Everyday Life.* Lincoln, NE: iUniverse.

Jones, B., & Iredale, N. (2009). Entrepreneurship education and Web 2.0. *Journal of Research in Marketing and Entrepreneurship, 11*(1), 66–77. doi: 10.1108/14715200911014158

Kim, J., Lee, J., Lee, H., & Paik, E. (2010). Design and implementation of the location-based personalized social media service. *2010 Fifth International*

Conference on Internet and Web Applications and Services (May), 116–121.

Lazaroiu, G. (2010). Social media, networking software, and creative digital marketing. *Review of Contemporary Philosophy, 9,* 160–165.

McGibbon, S., & Moutray, C. (2009). The small business economy: A report to the President. *United States Government Printing Office, 7–25.* Retrieved from http://www.sba.gov/advo/research/sb_econ2009.pdf

McMullen, J. S., & Shepherd, D. A. (2006). Entrepreneurial action and the role of uncertainty in the theory of the entrepreneur. *Academy of Management Review, 31*(1), 132–152.

Moustakas, C. (1994). *Phenomenological research methods.* Thousand Oaks, CA: Sage Publications.

Nissing, N. (2007). Would you buy a purple orange? *Research Technology Management, 50*(May/June), 35–39. Popkin, J., & Kobe, K. (2006). US manufacturing innovation at risk. *Material Handling & Logistics,* 1–62. Powers, T. L., & Leal, R. P. (1994). Is the U.S. innovative? A cross-national study of patent activity. *Management International Review, 34*(1), 67–78. Proctor, T. (2010). *Creative problem solving for managers: Developing skills for decision making and innovation* (3rd ed.). New York, NY: Taylor & Francis.

Sailer, K. (2011). Creativity as social and spatial process. *Facilities, 29*(1/2), 6–18. doi: 10.1108/02632771111101296

Schwab, K. (2009). *The global competitiveness report: 2009–2010.* Geneva, Switzerland: World Economic Forum. Retrieved from http://www3.weforum.org/docs/ WEF_GlobalCompetitivenessReport_2010–11.pdf

Shih, C.C. (2009). *The Facebook era: Tapping online social networks to build better products, reach new audiences, and sell more stuff:* Prentice Hall PTR.

Skinner, G. (2010). The I-CAN tool and managing information and communication technology (ICT) innovation in Australia. *Innovative Studies: International Journal (ISIJ), 1*(1), 1–18. Retrieved from http://www.cscjournals .org/csc/manuscriptinfo

Snyder, C. R., & Lopez, S. J. (2009). *Oxford handbook of positive psychology.* New York, NY: Oxford University Press.

Spahr, R. W. (2009). The root cause of the current financial crisis, effects on capital markets, and long-term solutions. *Business Perspectives, 19*(4), 42–45.

Sternberg, R. J. (2008). The WICS approach to leadership: Stories of leadership and the structures and processes that support them. *The Leadership Quarterly, 19,* 360–371. doi: 310.1016/j.leaqua.2008.1003.1008

U.S. Small Business Administration (SBA) Office of Advocacy. (2009). *The small business economy: A report to the President.* Retrieved March 19, 2010, from http://www.sba.gov/advo/research/sb_econ2009.pdf

Vickers, J. N. (2010). Discovering golf's innermost truths: A new approach to teaching the game. *International Journal of Sports Science and Coaching, 5(-*1), 89–93. doi: 10.1260/1747–9541.1265.s1262.1289

Wadhwa, V., Gereffi, G., Rissing, B., & Ong, R. (2007). Where the engineers are. *Issues in Science & Technology, 23*(3), 73–84.

Wallas, G. (1926). *The art of thought.* New York, NY: Harcourt.

Walumbwa, F., Avolio, B., & Zhu, W. (2008). How transformational leadership weaves its influence on individual job performance: The role of identification and efficacy beliefs. *Personnel Psychology, 61,* 793–825. doi: 710.1111/j.1744–6570.2008.00131.x

About the Author

Geographic Information Systems consultant and Syracuse, New Yorker native Nate Boyer holds several accredited degrees including: a Bachelor of Speech Communications(BA) from Syracuse University's School of Visual and Performing Arts, a Bachelors of Public Relations from Syracuse University's prestigious S.I. Newhouse School of Public Communications (BA), a Master of Science (MS) in Technology Management from the University of Maryland University College with a concentration in Entrepreneurship and Innovation, and a Doctorate of Business Administration (DBA) from University of Phoenix School of Advanced Studies. Nate's dissertation was entitled: *A Phenomenological Study: How motivation and Creativity Influence Small Internet Entrepreneurs' Innovations.*

For over 20 years, Dr. Nate has worked in the aerospace and defense industry and the geographic information systems field. Dr. Nate formerly served as General Manager and Director of World Wide Sales at Eastman Kodak's Commercial Remote Sensing & Images as Information division, managing several multi-million dollar defense satellite systems and commercial earth observation programs. Dr. Nate has held the position of director of commercial remote sensing technology at Boeing's Integrated Defense Systems unit as well as managed government programs for Lockheed Martin's Earth Observation Satellite Company. Dr. Nate is currently a geographic information systems consultant in upstate New York, specializing in satellite imagery, aerial photography and 3D visualization.

To reach Dr. Nate for information on entrepreneurship, innovation, or any of these topics, please contact him via email at setsuccess@aol.com

MIXED METHOD

CHAPTER 7

A Mixed Method Analysis to Refine an Organizational Change Model for Technology Organizations

Dr. Leigh Riley

It's all about the journey! This is a chant to keep in mind throughout the entire dissertation process: to include choosing the right methodology and design elements that will accomplish the purpose of the study and demonstrate what the IRB/ARB needs to see. Whether trying to solve world hunger, an industry issue, or addressing a passion, a myriad of designs are available for a research study. This chapter reviews the methodology Riley (2010) used in her dissertation for a doctorial program in Organizational Management/Information Systems and Technology.

The study conducted in 2010 for the dissertation of Riley (2010), used an exploratory mixed method research approach that combined content analysis, quantitative survey design, and comparative analysis to refine an organizational change model (The Protean Model®) developed through personal experience and research. The use of a mixed method certainly increased the amount of work needed to complete a dissertation. However, the results proved insightful; provided a type of validation for The Protean Model® that is accepted by technology workers; and supports a comprehensive, yet practical approach to implementing organizational change.

AN OVERVIEW OF THE SITUATION

Maximizing profit is a primary goal of many organizations. To accomplish this goal, leaders must have reliable information as the basis for decisions to commit organizational assets to endeavors that yield the best returns on investment. In addition, these leaders must make decisions that also develop and maintain their competitive edge in the marketplace. Organization's leaders face the necessity for change in today's business environment. Such change requires agility to take advantage of changes in the market trends, the financial environment, and their industry's direction. Agile organizations change by learning and adopting new organizational behaviors. Agile organizations learn to provide high quality, low-cost products and services, while establishing a differentiating position in the marketplace that attracts and retains customers.

For military or government systems and software contractors, adopting a CMMI®-DEV model to improve their software development processes and obtain a CMMI®-DEV maturity level rating is a differentiator that may increase their ability to accrue contracts and market share. To obtain a CMMI®-DEV maturity level rating an organization must transform the organization and the software development group's policies, processes, and behavior (Ahern, Armstrong, Clouse, Ferguson, Hayes, & Nidiffer, 2005). This transformation is a complex undertaking and requires a holistic organizational change approach to be successful.

According to Burke and Burke (2008), there are commonalities in the holistic approach among organizations who successfully engaged in change, yet each organization's approach is different. This holistic approach to change includes common elements such as managing the effort from the top, planning the change, and incorporating the very foundation of the organization in the change (Burke & Burke, 2008). Without a systematic and holistic organizational change model incorporating these key elements, change can negatively affect an organization in many different ways, including increased implementation cost and time, organization stress, and risk that the organization fails to achieve the goals of the change effort.

Accordingly, this problem also applies to the many private sector organizations and public sector institutions and agencies that implement CMMI®. The specific problem they face is that organizations implementing CMMI® do so without a project management-based organizational change model that will mitigate the negative effects caused by such a broad transformation of their organizational processes and behavior. Organizational leaders typically spend 2% to 6% of their information technology (IT) budget for software process improvement efforts like CMMI® (Reitzig, 2005). To make such a significant investment, decision makers should "understand how specific resource commitments for IT result in improved outputs and outcomes" (Rivenbark, Fitzgerald, & Schelin, 2003, p. 497).

Data on the organizational change factors for implementation of CMMI®-DEV processes is prolific yet chaotic; most of the data is either anecdotal or has not been collected under the discipline of an empirical study. Many presentations and articles exist that describe the factors contributing to the success of CMMI®-DEV implementations. However, researchers have not adequately analyzed and identified which organizational change factors contribute most to the ability of a company's employees to implement successfully the CMMI®-DEV model.

The Riley (2010) study analyzed the myriad of presentations and articles, as well as surveyed process improvement practitioners implementing the CMMI®-DEV, or those affected by an implementation. This triangulation of data sources narrowed the broad list of organizational change factors necessary for a successful implementation of process improvements using the CMMI®-DEV. In addition, process improvement leaders can use the Riley (2010) study results to create a strategy that can increase the probability for successfully implementing changes in their organization.

REVIEW OF THE METHODOLOGY

Riley (2010) employed an exploratory mixed methodology and design for the study. Its purpose was to (a) determine the organizational change factors indicative of success of implementation of the CMMI®-DEV; (b) compare the results of the content analysis with surveys of the perceptions of leaders and practitioners who have implemented the CMMI®-DEV model; and (c) refine The Protean Model® to support change initiatives within technology organizations. This was accomplished by using content analysis and descriptive statistics. Using data from several different sources and data collection techniques, to include the broadest range of perspectives for the study, expanded the understanding of the data obtained by these multiple methods (Creswell, 2003). The organizational change factors were identified through a survey instrument and an analysis of keywords within presentations and published articles. The identified organizational change factors were then used to refine The Protean Model®.

The exploratory mixed method approach in the Riley (2010) study consisted of three phases. The first two phases (content analysis and survey) were conducted to combine qualitative and quantitative approaches to uncover factors associated with successful CMMI®-DEV implementations and to refine The Protean Model®. According to Creswell et al. (2004), a mixed method research design adds rigor to the research by combining transformation of data, instrument design, and triangulation.

Transformation of the data from the presentations and articles was done using a qualitative content analysis approach. Content analysis, according to Neuman (2005), is a technique that compares various textual artifacts and determines themes across those artifacts. Descriptive statistics, a quantitative technique, was then used on the survey data to provide credibility to the Riley (2010) study and support its ability to be replicated in future studies (Marsland, Wilson, Abeyasekera, & Klieh, 2009).

The content analysis and descriptive statistics results provided the data necessary to triangulate and then compare against the prescriptions in The Protean Model® and to determine if changes or refinements to that model were necessary. Figure 1 illustrates the high level processes that were used in the Riley (2010) study. By using both quantitative and qualitative research methods, a researcher can combine triangulation, instrument design, and transformation of data to add rigor to the research (Creswell, Fetters, & Ivankova, 2004).

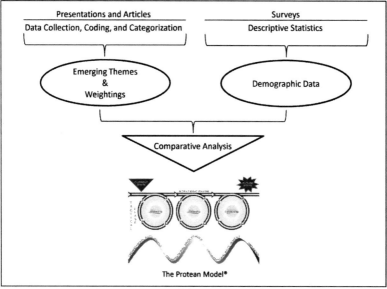

Figure 1. Representation of the Process of This Exploratory Mixed Methods Research.

The first phase of the Riley (2010) study was a content analysis to explore the prevalence of the organizational change factors that support successful implementation of a specific process improvement initiative as mentioned in the published presentations and articles. In addition, the content analysis determined the measurement of each of the organizational change factors. Content analysis is a technique used in both qualitative and quantitative research to analyze the content of text (i.e., books, transcripts, and movies). According to Neuman (2005), "in content analysis, a researcher uses objective and systematic counting and recording procedures to produce a quantitative description of the symbolic content in a text" (p. 311). Additionally, content analysis allows a researcher to "compare content across many texts and analyze it with quantitative techniques (for example, charts and tables)" (Neuman, 2005, p. 311).

A content analysis approach provided a practical view, from textual records, of the factors that affect a successful implementation of a particular process improvement model. The presentations and articles were from the Software Engineering Process Group (SEPG) and National Defense Industrial Association (NDIA) conference proceedings and the *CrossTalk* Journal. The content analysis uncovered themes about organizational change factors supporting successful process improvement initiatives. Organizational factors have an effect on change initiatives, making it important for Riley to identify those factors supporting business leaders' decision making on the planning and execution of the change initiative. The database for the search of keywords was generated based on the guidance in The Protean Model®. The content analysis keyword statistics were descriptive and not inferential since the data was generated by a keyword textual search across the publications studied and not an in-depth analysis of them individually. The mention of a keyword term was only highlighted, so this search did not capture the tone of the publication, nor the complete context or the author's perspective in detail. These limitations led the researcher to be very conservative in using tests upon this data that could have led to overly confident conclusions.

The second phase of the Riley (2010) study was quantitative, using a survey and descriptive statistics to explain further the context in which the organizational change factors were identified and to assign scores and rank order them. The descriptive statistics summarized the population demographic data, such as the size of the organization, maturity level, number of years in process improvement, and percentage of budget used for process improvement. Descriptive statistics are useful to summarize trends or tendencies in data and help to provide an understanding of how one score compares to other scores (Creswell, 2005). Descriptive statistics "indicate general tendencies in the data (mean, mode, median), the spread of scores (variance, standard deviation, and range), or a comparison of how one score relates to all others (z-scores, percentile rank)" (Creswell, 2005, p. 181).

The purpose of descriptive statistics is to describe and record information about the characteristics of the participants rather than determine an association between the information that is collected (Cozby, 2008). In other words, descriptive statistics were useful to compile an accurate description of the characteristics of the participants in the Riley (2010) study as well as their perceptions and opinions. Including descriptive statistics provides credibility to the analysis because the results and findings could be replicable for future studies (Marsland et al., 2009). In the Riley (2010) study, trends in descriptive statistics, including the numbers, percentages, and proportions of participants responding to each of the survey questions were useful to document the credibility and to create a replicable study. Therefore, a comparison of the results from the Riley (2010) study with results from other studies in the same or similar fields, to determine whether the results are consistent, are possible.

The third phase of the Riley (2010) study was a comparative analysis to refine The Protean Model®, developed through personal experience and research. The comparative analysis phase of the study used data from the content analysis and survey. Riley used this data to compare against the guidelines recommended in The Protean Model® and determine if the model should be changed and determine if the model reflects real-world practices. In order for The Protean Model® to reflect real-world practices, Riley refined it using the answers to the following research questions:

RQ1. What organizational change factors contribute to a successful implementation of CMMI®-based process improvement initiatives?

RQ2. Does the ranking, by order of importance, of the organizational change factors vary with the maturity level of the organization?

RQ3. Does the ranking, by order of importance, of the organizational change factors vary with the size of the organization?

RQ4. Does the ranking, by order of importance, of the organizational change factors vary with the percentage of budget expended on software process improvement?

RQ5. Does the ranking, by order of importance, of the organizational change factors vary with the number of months in process improvement?

RQ6. Do the organizational change factors identified in The Protean Model® correspond with those factors identified with the success of CMMI®-based process improvement initiatives?

POPULATION AND SAMPLING

In order to adequately address the research questions, Riley selected a specific population from which to gather data. The members of the Riley (2010) study population had varying levels of experience and included managers, process improvement leads, and practitioners affiliated with organizations that develop software and have conducted a CMMI®-DEV SCAMPI[SM] appraisal.

The population for a study, as defined by Mendenhall, Beaver, and Beaver (2008), is the group of subjects or participants to which inferences and conclusions are to be drawn.

The sample for the content analysis phase of the Riley (2010) study included 80 presentations and articles published during the period 2002–2009. Managers, process improvement leads, and practitioners in companies that have implemented CMMI® authored articles and presentations analyzed in the content analysis phase. The 69 survey participants were solicited from the attendees at an annual conference specific to the CMMI® process improvement industry (SEPG North America, 2010). In addition, potential participants were solicited through various LinkedIn groups with relevance to process improvement and CMMI®. Participants voluntarily chose to participate.

For the purposes of the Riley (2010) study, a convenience-sampling plan was used. The convenience-sampling plan is a form of non-probability sampling in which the participants are selected as they come along (Urdan, 2005). A convenience sampling plan has the advantage of enabling the researcher to obtain more data points in a shorter period of time, as opposed to a probability sampling technique such as random sampling (Cozby, 2008). The increased quantity of data points was important to this study because it provided the ability to generalize the outcomes to other groups. Similarly, the convenience-sampling plan was appropriate for the Riley (2010) study because the members of different organizations were not randomly selected from the entire population of employees within the organizations.

The content analysis and survey sample size was sufficient because it was large enough to give the researcher an adequate measure of the organizational change factors that may affect implementation of the CMMI®-DEV model. In general, qualitative studies usually do not require a large number of participants unless they are very complex (Marshall, 1996). Marshall (1996) indicated that, "the number of required subjects usually becomes obvious as the current study progresses, as new categories, themes or explanations stop emerging from the data" (p. 523). Therefore, this means that a smaller sample size of participants would be as beneficial as a larger sample for the context of the Riley (2010) study.

INSTRUMENTATION

For the second phase of the study, Riley (2010) designed a survey to explore the context in which the organizational change factors occurred. The survey had two sections: the first section contained questions regarding the participants' organization and their role and the second section contained questions regarding the participants' perception of the organizational change factors that contribute to successful process improvement initiatives.

All sections of the survey, named *Process Improvement Cultural Assessment* (PICA), were developed for the study. Prior to conducting the second phase, a pilot survey was conducted using a representative group of respondents. The pilot questionnaire was distributed to a group of 10–30 participants who were employees within different organizations. Representative sets of participants were selected from the target population for the pilot. The individuals who participated in the pilot were not included in the final sample collected for study.

The consistency of the results between the pilot and the survey indicated that the survey instrument reliably measured the perception of the organizational change factor's effect on CMMI® implementation success. Reliability is defined as the consistency of measurement in the repeated application of the measuring device (Tashakkori & Teddlie, 1998). Riley (2010) estimated the reliability of the PICA by using a test/retest method consistent with this definition.

DATA COLLECTION, VALIDITY, AND RELIABILITY

Data collection processes were different for each phase of the study. The content analysis phase used data from presentations given at the SEPG and NDIA conferences, and downloaded articles from *CrossTalk* magazine's online database. To convert the content of the articles and presentations into precise and quantifiable data, a codebook was defined to allow the researcher to collect valid measurement data and replicate the analysis. The codebook was developed using NVivo8® quantitative computer software. The data collected was sorted into categories and entered into a searchable keyword database for the content analysis. Sorting data into categories allowed the emergence of patterns and themes regarding factors that support successful process improvement initiatives.

Subsequently, quantitative data for the study was collected using a survey instrument distributed to the potential participants. The survey consisted of a combination of closed-ended or forced answer questions using yes and no responses, multiple-choice responses, or a 6-point Likert scale. A consideration in the design of the survey instrument was the number of points on the scale. According to Bartram (2007), a problem with 'forced choice' Likert scales is that such scales tend to positively skew the overall results. In such a forced choice situation, respondents prefer to 'be nice,' and chose to rate items positively rather than negatively, i.e., choosing 'somewhat agree' rather than 'somewhat disagree' (Bartram, 2007). The overwhelming majority of "agree" versus "disagree" answers received to many of the survey questions may be the result of a 'Halo effect' and the respondents may have given high or low ratings to all factors with an overall feeling of like or dislike. Riley (2010) chose a 6-point Likert scale; each response ranging from *strongly disagree* to *strongly agree* corresponded to a score of 1, 2, 3, 4, 5, or 6 points. The Likert scale was useful to determine how strongly the respondent of a question agrees with a concise statement (Delaney, 2004). According to Converse and Presser (1986), in a survey designed with no middle category the researcher loses information from the participants about the direction in which they lean (p. 37). In an analysis of Likert item responses, a value of the overall responses can be calculated based on a 6-point scale wherein the closer the number is to 6, the more the response indicates agreement. Because of the type of questions (forced answer or closed-ended), the responses were more easily quantifiable, making a comparison to determine relationships among participants' responses possible.

The participants accessed the survey instrument for the Riley (2010) study online. The URL for the survey website was sent via discussion group postings and flyers. According to Wright (2005), researchers have increasingly used the Internet and online surveys in research over the past decade. In addition, recent developments in survey authoring software and online survey services have reduced the amount of labor and time required to produce quality surveys. This study used the online survey service QuestionPro. One of the advantages of using online surveys in the current research project was the ability to reach the survey participants located across the United States. Using an online survey also facilitated automated data collection, reducing the time needed to complete the research. Some of the disadvantages of online surveys "include uncertainty over the validity of the data and sampling issues, and concerns surrounding the design, implementation, and evaluation of an online survey" (Wright, 2005, p. 2).

To draw useful conclusions and increase the validity and reliability of the Riley (2010) study it was important to minimize any compromises in the design. Carmines and Zeller (1979) defined validity as an "interpretation of data arising from a specified procedure" (p. 17). Researchers refer to reliability meaning that a test produces consistent results after repeated uses (Carmines & Zeller, 1979). Strauss and Corbin (2008) contended that when discussing qualitative research, reliability and validity "indicates that findings are trustworthy and believable in that they reflect participants', researchers', and readers' experiences with a phenomenon" (p. 302). The validity and reliability of the PICA instrument was determined by comparing the survey data with the data from the content analysis. The comparison of the data showed a similar ranking of the organizational change factors, supporting the presumption that the PICA instrument was reliable.

Internal validity can be achieved when "scores from an instrument are . . . internally consistent across items on the instrument" (Creswell, 2005, p. 164). Consistency for the PICA instrument was tested in two different ways: a Kuder-Richardson split half test and a coefficient alpha. External validity is the researcher's ability to generalize the results to groups outside the current study. Choosing participants who closely match those of the target population of the study and ensuring their participation by making it as convenient as possible to the participants can improve external validity. This was accomplished by using a web-based distribution of the survey (via QuestionPro) and collection of the responses.

ANALYSIS OF THE DATA

In the first phase of the Riley (2010) study, the content analysis phase, various textual data sources were summarized and compared to confirm the organizational change factors in implementing CMMI®-based process improvements. The information from the texts and articles was categorized based on similarities between the sentence structures and words. The NVivo8® data analysis program, a contemporary software program designed for qualitative research, was used to record, assess, and analyze the text of the articles and presentations.

Textual keyword matches were coded and recorded as cases with the NVivo software and then summarized for further analysis.

Because the researcher created the organizational change model being refined, an outside analyst developed the code used in the content analysis. This removed the bias from the content analysis coding that may have existed. The results from the program were summarized and measurements developed based on the frequency of responses using the codes assigned during the codification process.

In the second phase of the study, the data analysis tools used on the information collected from the survey instruments, were summary statistics. The analysis was conducted using Microsoft Excel's statistical add-in. The descriptive statistics computed for the study included frequency distributions as well as measures of central tendency. The analysis was limited to calculating the means, standard deviations, and variances of the sample responses using a scaling method to transform them from ordinal to interval measures. This very conservative approach mitigated the potential to draw overly confident conclusions.

PRESENTATION OF DATA FINDINGS

The organizational change factors from the content analysis phase were assigned a numerical score based on the number of occurrences (mentions) of the keywords within the 80 articles and presentations and then ranked highest to lowest (see Table 1). These keywords either matched the words used in the survey question exactly or were the closest reasonable synonym. This ranking of the numerical scores showed there was a substantial gap between the score of the topmost and the lowest ranked organizational change factors.

TABLE 1. *ORGANIZATIONAL CHANGE FACTOR RANKING FROM CONTENT ANALYSIS RESULTS*

Question in Ranked Order	Total
Providing support mechanisms (infrastructure, processes, tools, etc.) is important to the success of a process improvement initiative.	129
Aligning the organization's process improvement initiative with its strategic goals is important to the success of a process improvement initiative.	42
Communication is important to the success of a process improvement initiative.	29
Managing the process improvement initiative as a project (planning, budget, schedule, oversight, etc.) is important to the success of a process improvement initiative.	29
Periodic and consistent measuring of progress is important to the success of a process improvement initiative.	18
Involving employees both inside and outside of the actual process improvement project, during the planning and implementation activities, is important to the success of a process improvement initiative.	13
Training the leadership team (senior and operational) is important to the success of a process improvement initiative.	8
Clearly articulating the benefits of the process improvement initiative to all employees is important to the success of a process improvement initiative.	8
Changing the employee (all employees, to include leadership) performance management system is important to the success of a process improvement initiative.	7
Incremental, instead of 'big bang' improvements are important to the success of a process improvement initiative.	5
Training the employees (those affected by the process improvement initiative) is important to the success of a process improvement initiative.	3
Senior leadership support is important to the success of a process improvement initiative.	1
Operational leadership (e.g., program management and project management) is important to the success of a process improvement initiative.	1

Survey participants identified and ranked organizational change factors based on a weighted scale of responses (see Table 2). The respondents agreed that every one of the factors were important and no respondent answered "disagree" or below to any of the questions. The distribution of the weighted score had a mean, variance, and standard deviation of 381.46, 548.71, and 23.42 respectively.

TABLE 2. ORGANIZATIONAL CHANGE FACTOR RANKING FROM SURVEY RESULTS

Question in Ranked Order	Weighted Factor
Senior leadership support is important to the success of a process improvement initiative.	408
Communication is important to the success of a process improvement initiative.	406
Training the employees (those affected by the process improvement initiative) is important to the success of a process improvement initiative.	397
Periodic and consistent measuring of progress is important to the success of a process improvement initiative.	394
Operational leadership (e.g., program management and project management) is important to the success of a process improvement initiative.	393
Aligning the organization's process improvement initiative with its strategic goals is important to the success of a process improvement initiative.	388
Managing the process improvement initiative as a project (planning, budget, schedule, oversight, etc.) is important to the success of a process improvement initiative.	383
Training the leadership team (senior and operational) is important to the success of a process improvement initiative.	382
Providing support mechanisms (infrastructure, processes, tools, etc.) is important to the success of a process improvement initiative.	382

Clearly articulating the benefits of the process improvement initiative to all employees is important to the success of a process improvement initiative.	380
Incremental, instead of 'big bang' improvements are important to the success of a process improvement initiative.	374
Involving employees both inside and outside of the actual process improvement project, during the planning and implementation activities, is important to the success of a process improvement initiative.	359
Changing the employee (all employees, to include leadership) performance management system is important to the success of a process improvement initiative.	313

Comparative analysis of both the content analysis and survey data confirmed that the organizational change factors identified in The Protean Model® contributed to the success of CMMI®-based process improvement initiatives (see Table 3). The importance of each organizational change factor differed between each of the data collections; however all of the organizational change factors were noted positively.

TABLE 3. *IDENTIFICATION OF THE ORGANIZATIONAL CHANGE FACTORS*

The Protean Model® Factors	Organizational Change Factors Identified	
	Survey	Content Analysis
Communication	Yes	Yes
Senior Leadership Support	Yes	Yes
Operational Leadership	Yes	Yes
Managing Initiative as a Project	Yes	Yes
Training the Leadership	Yes	Yes
Training the Employees	Yes	Yes
Measuring of Progress	Yes	Yes

Changing the Performance Management System	Yes	Yes
Providing Support Mechanisms	Yes	Yes
Articulating the Benefits	Yes	Yes
Involving Employees	Yes	Yes
Aligning the Initiative with Strategic Goals	Yes	Yes
Incremental Improvements	Yes	Yes

The findings in the study indicated there was an agreement on the list of organizational change factors associated with successful CMMI® implementations. In addition, the ranking in order of importance of the organizational change factors across data sources paralleled each other. The organizational change factor ranking varied according to demographics. While there were differences in the rankings of the organizational change factors, these differences were not noteworthy within the scope of the study's analysis.

This research confirmed The Protean Model®'s emphasis on organizational change factors affecting the outcome of CMMI®-based process improvement initiatives. This was demonstrated by the general and uniform agreement expressed by the survey respondents on the relative importance of several organizational change factors (i.e., communication, senior leadership support, measuring progress, training employees, and operational leadership). However, comparison with the content analysis-based ranking of the same organizational change factors differed in several respects. Those differences could not be fully explained due to the limitations inherent in the content analysis approach. For example, the presentations and articles reviewed contained the organizational change factor "keywords", but the full context of those keyword references could not be directly compared with the survey response data.

DRAWING CONCLUSIONS

The literature review for the Riley (2010) study included a discussion of several organizational change theories as they apply to technology companies. The predominant models are TQM, BPR, and CMMI®. CMMI®-DEV is a framework for affecting organizational change at the operational level of a software development organization, which is driven by decisions from leaders. Leaders use tactical decision models to implement strategic decisions and generate the impetus of change. The literature review led the researcher to consider how organizational change and process improvement initiatives, such as CMMI®, are related to both strategic decisions and tactical planning.

Contingency theorists posit that there is no best way to lead or organize a company and no best way to make decisions. Decision-making, leadership styles, and organizational change are dependent on internal and external situational factors. After a review of the broader body of literature, it is clear that The Protean Model® fits within the contingency theory framework for organizational change, as discussed by (Lawrence & Lorsch, 1967; Woodward, 1965). The basis of The Protean Model®'s framework is a consideration of the contingencies in making tactical decisions for an organizational change effort.

The approach taken to research situational models of organizational change and decision-making involved asking current leaders and practitioners to share their perceptions and to rank several organizational change factors, such as communication, planning, measurement, and leadership. The organizational change factors were identified from the prescriptive guidance in The Protean Model®. The qualitative phase of the Riley (2010) study was a content analysis which reviewed 80 published presentations and journal articles on CMMI® process improvement initiatives.

In the content analysis phase, the organizational change factors were ranked according to the number of times they were mentioned in the articles and presentations. The content analysis results showed the ranking of the top five organizational change factors instrumental in the success of CMMI® process improvement initiatives to be: providing support mechanisms, align the initiative with strategic goals, communication, managing the initiative as a project, and measuring of progress. The frequency of mention for the next six organizational change factors (involving employees, training the leadership, articulating the benefits, changing the performance management system, incremental improvements, and training the employees) was much less than in the top five. The two organizational change factors that were ranked at the bottom were: senior leadership support and operational leadership.

For the quantitative phase of the Riley (2010) study, a survey instrument was created and distributed to a select group of leaders and practitioners of CMMI® process improvement initiatives. The survey questions were designed to isolate responses and categorize the respondents' degree of agreement or disagreement with the significance of this set of organizational change factors. While leaders and practitioners agreed on the organizational change factors, the order in which they ranked those organizational change factors in the survey results differed from the rankings in the content analysis.

According to the survey results, the respondents agreed that the ranking of the top five organizational change factors (senior leadership support, communication, measuring of progress, training the employees, and operational leadership) were instrumental in the success of CMMI® process improvement initiatives. The ranking of the next 6 organizational change factors (managing the initiative as a project, training the leadership, align the initiative with strategic goals, articulating the benefits, providing support mechanisms, and incremental improvements) was not as consistent across the group of respondents. There were two organizational change factors (changing the performance management system and involving employees) that were consistently ranked at the bottom. The difference in the rankings might be due to the differences in the situational environments of the various survey participants and authors of the presentations and articles. These differences could signify the justification for using a situational prescriptive model like The Protean Model® when affecting change in an organization.

The results of the Riley (2010) study are important to process improvement leaders and practitioners as a source of guidance and insight into the organizational change factors that support a successful CMMI® implementation. By applying the study results, decision makers can focus on the organizational change factors that are the most influential in determining the success of their initiative. The cost of process improvement initiatives is sizeable. Providing leaders with information that minimizes the risks of implementation failure will benefit the stakeholders, the end users, and the practitioners and sponsors.

Organizational change decision makers and stakeholders face major challenges ensuring the success and sustainability of their process improvement initiatives because the risks, as well as the initiative's direct and indirect costs, can be substantial. However, the magnitude of those costs is just one measure to consider and does not include the less tangible, but no less important costs arising from the loss of strategic advantage and other competitive and financial opportunities resulting from an initiative's failure.

The value of The Protean Model®'s refined prescription of organizational change factors is twofold. First, the model can be a tool leaders use to reduce the process improvement initiative's inherent costs and risks. Second, identifying the ranking of the controllable organizational change factors can help leaders prioritize the scope and resource allocation decisions. The Protean Model® is a guide for the members of this audience in achieving their process improvement initiative goals with greater certainty by reducing the influence of subjective judgments and perceptions.

The number of organizations and firms undertaking organizational change and process improvement initiatives continues to grow. The accumulation of knowledge and experience arising from these efforts should be captured and analyzed to improve and revise the current theoretical frameworks and the models based upon those frameworks. As the number of organizations and initiatives increases, the outcomes should be analyzed and that data from the successful initiatives should be used to enhance the ranking of the controllable organizational change factors. This type of information would be of great benefit to the leaders and practitioners of the CMMI® process improvement community.

The leaders and practitioners of the process improvement community need to: (a) share more detailed information about their process improvement initiative outcomes with the goal of creating and then refining organizational change models; (b) create better methods and tailored initiative prototypes that can serve as guides to reduce costs and risks of organizational change; and (c) communicate the reported organizational change factors and use surveys and other tools to develop organizational change factor rankings.

Further research is needed to define the success of organizational change initiatives within technology organizations. The categorization of organizational change factors runs into immediate difficulties due to subjectivity and a lack of consensus as to the specific meaning for each of the terms. Differing perspectives of success and failure result in conflicting and inconsistent recommendations (Lyytinen & Hirschheim, 1987; Sauer, 1993). The proportion of these change initiatives that fail is unknown and without further evaluation, the degree to which these organizational change factors were present cannot be determined.

The degree of correlation between the survey and content analysis organizational change factors with the demographic characteristics of the participating firms requires further study. The variance in organizational change factor ranking for firms of differing sizes, maturity levels, expenditure of budget, and time in process improvement requires further investigation so that unique profiles can be developed to support decision making by leaders of the various organization situational contexts.

The traceability of the organizational change factors to specific outcomes (such as the achievement of a particular maturity level) that would allow decision makers to allocate resources appropriately is lacking and requires further analysis and study. Budgets for organizational change initiatives remain a risky investment until a cause and effect model can be developed to guide project management decision-making.

Organizational change is a multi-dimensional decision problem: decision makers struggle to arrive at the correct combination of strategic and tactical approaches for their specific organizational context. The mixed method approach in the Riley (2010) study provided the tools necessary to explore this problem from multiple perspectives and combine the survey responses and themes from the content analysis, arriving at a holistic insight into this complex phenomenon. Technology organizations wanting to improve their performance, internally and externally, need practical guidance to achieve greater flexibility and market potential. The results of the research will allow Riley to create a practical, yet holistic, set of processes that support The Protean Model®'s framework. This framework will contribute to a better understanding of how to conduct successful organizational change initiatives.

REFERENCES

Ahern, D., Armstrong, J., Clouse, A., Ferguson, J., Hayes, W., & Nidiffer, K. (2005). *CMMI® distilled: Appraisals for process improvement*. Upper Saddle River, NJ: Addison-Wesley.

Bartram, D. (2007). Increasing validity with forced-choice criterion measurement formats. *International Journal of Selection and Assessment, 15*(3), 263–272.

Burke, W., & Burke, W. (2008). *Organization change: Theory and practice*. Thousand Oaks, CA: Sage Publications.

Carmines, E., & Zeller, R. (1979). *Reliability and validity assessment*. Thousand Oaks, CA: Sage Publications.

Converse, J., & Presser, S. (1986). *Survey questions: Handcrafting the standardized questionnaire*. Thousand Oaks, CA: Sage Publications.

Cozby, P. (2008). *Methods in behavioral research*. New York, NY: McGraw-Hill.

Creswell, J. (2003). *Research design: Qualitative, quantitative, and mixed methods approaches* (2nd ed.). Thousand Oaks, CA: Sage Publications.

Creswell, J. (2005). *Educational research: Planning, conducting, and evaluating quantitative and qualitative research* (2nd ed.). Upper Saddle River, NJ: Pearson.

Creswell, J., Fetters, M., & Ivankova, N. (2004). Designing a mixed methods study in primary care. *Annals of Family Medicine, 2*(1), 7–12.

Delaney, T. (2004). *Likert scale*. Retrieved from http://www.isixsigma.com/ dictionary/Likert_Scale-588.htm.

Lawrence, P., & Lorsch, J. (1967). Differentiation and integration in complex organizations. *Administrative Science Quarterly, 12*, 1–30.

Lyytinen, K., & Hirschheim, R. (1987). Information system failures: A survey and classification of the empirical literature. *Oxford Surveys in Information Technology, 4*, 257–309.

Marshall, M. (1996). Sampling for qualitative research. *Family Practice, 13*(6), 522–526.

Marsland, N., Wilson, I., Abeyasekera, S., & Klieh, L. (2009). A methodological framework for combining qualitative and quantitative survey methods. Retrieved from http://www.reading.ac.uk/ssc/publications/guides/qqa.pdf.

Mendenhall, W., Beaver, R., & Beaver, B. (2008). *Introduction to probability and statistics.* Pacific Grove, CA: Duxbury Press.

Neuman, W. (2005). *Social research methods: Qualitative and quantitative approaches* (6th ed.). Upper Saddle River, NJ: Prentice Hall.

Reitzig, R. (2005, November). *CMMI® process improvement—It's not a technical problem, it's a people problem!* Paper presented at the meeting of the CMMI® Technology Conference and Users Group, Denver, CO.

Riley, L. (2010). *A mixed method analysis to refine an organizational change model for technology organizations.* (Unpublished doctoral dissertation). University of Phoenix, Phoenix, AZ.

Rivenbark, W., Fitzgerald, K., & Schelin, S. (2003). Analyzing information technology investments in state government. *Social Science Computer Review, 21*(4), 497–505.

Sauer, C. (1993). *Why information systems fail: A case study approach.* Henley, UK: Alfred Waller.

Strauss, A., & Corbin, J. (2008). *Basics of qualitative research: Techniques and procedures for developing grounded theory* (3rd ed.). London, UK: Sage Publications.

Tashakkori, A., & Teddlie, C. (1998). *Mixed methodology: Combining qualitative and quantitative approaches.* Thousand Oaks, CA: Sage Publications.

Urdan, T. (2005). *Statistics in plain English.* Mahwah, NJ: Lawrence Erlbaum Associates.

Woodward, J. (1965). *Industrial organization.* London, England: Oxford Press.

Wright, K. (2005). Researching Internet-based populations: Advantages and disadvantages of online survey research, online questionnaire authoring software packages, and web survey services. *Journal of Computer-Mediated Communication, 10*(3). doi: 10.1111/j.1083–6101.2005.tb00259.x

About the Author

Dr. Leigh Riley is an SEI Certified SCAMPI[SM] Lead Appraiser. She is also the president/CEO of Acme Process Group, Paradigm Audit Services, and Pinnacle Systems Group. She resides in Northern VA with her husband and two Basenji puppies (Beau and Arrow). A graduate of the University of Phoenix, she earned a BS in Project Management, an MBA in Technology Management, and Doctorate in Organizational Management/Information Systems and Technology.

Dr. Leigh's research focuses on organizational change in technology firms, with an emphasis on her multi-dimensional change strategy called The Protean Model®. Dr. Leigh's 27 years experience in the IT industry has provided insight in working with organizations in reengineering and/or developing business processes and leading organizational change. This experience gave Dr. Leigh the vision for developing The Protean Model® and the passion to validate the model through her dissertation work.

Dr. Leigh teaches at Chancellor University and her dissertation results were recently presented at the 2010 Annual NDIA conference in Denver, CO.

Dr. Leigh Riley can be reached at drleighriley@gmail.com

CHAPTER 8

A Quantitative Correlational Analysis That Really Should Have Been a Mixed Study

Dr. Patricia M. Dues

When numeric data is being collected from a large number of individuals with a survey instrument customized for the study, a quantitative research method is typically appropriate. In this case, the approach should include preset questions designed to obtain data regarding the relationship among the variables with no predetermined effect identified. As the data is both numerical and measurable, it can be analyzed and the results related back to the hypotheses tested (Neuman, 2006).

However, research methodology is not always as "cut and dried" as initially thought to be. Sometimes the type of participants, their job responsibilities, size of the organization, industry specialty, or just a lack of interest in the study may have an impact on the success of the research methodology. Researchers need to be prepared to "think on their feet" and adapt to the situation presented, modify the approach, but stay in line with the specified method. This chapter presents an example of a study that met the requirements of a quantitative correlational analysis; but as the end results show, a mixed method study may have been a more appropriate approach.

DATA ANALYSIS METHODOLOGY

A correlational research design describes a relationship between two or more variables without directly attributing effect of one variable on another with the intent of identifying the direction and degree of association among the variables (Creswell, 2008). Correlations can reflect a direct or positive relationship among the variables, or be the opposite. As a result of correlational research, a linear relationship among the variables is analyzed.

In 2009, a study was conducted of US government technology leaders. The quantitative, correlational study examined the degree to which a relationship existed among the independent variables of leadership style and type of ERP implemented, and the dependent variable, perceived ERP success, in local government technology leaders (Dues, 2010). A quantitative research method was used that involved the collection of numerical data that assessed each variable of the study (Neuman, 2006). A search for correlations was planned to identify relationships among the variables of the study could be identified as a result of the data analysis (Creswell, 2008).

However, study results are only as good as the data collected. If the study population is geographically widespread; if the participants are from a specialized field and at an executive level of an organization; and if the size of the organization varies greatly among the population; collecting data may be a challenge. In this case the focus of data collection needs to be adjusted to include: (a) gaining the attention of the study population which may include a group of extremely busy executives; (b) accurately measuring the variables; (c) developing and testing an appropriate survey instrument; and (d) establishing various data collection channels.

GAINING THE ATTENTION OF THE STUDY POPULATION

For a study population that is situated over a large geographical area, extremely busy in their profession, or that need to feel secure in the anonymity of their responses, completing an Internet-based survey is the best approach. Numerous individuals from the targeted industry can be invited to participate in the study. A link to the Internet survey site can be provided for access to the survey. Calculating the sample size for the study is critical. It should be based on a combination of confidence interval, likely response rate, and standard sampling error. In the Dues (2010) dissertation study, the standard values for significance level represented by α were set at 5% and 1%. When $\alpha = .05$, a 0.95 or 95% probability exists of a correct statistical conclusion when the null hypothesis is true and is equivalent to a 95% confidence level to reject H0 (Aczel & Sounderpandian, 2009).

In the study of US government technology leaders a random sample was developed based on the target sample guidelines (Dues, 2010). A 50% chance that the leaders surveyed have implemented an ERP system, a 10% potential sampling error, and a 95% confidence interval, resulted in a target sample size of approximately 100 technology leaders throughout the U.S. (Creswell, 2008). Three databases were identified for the sample population: (a) a metropolitan organization of 58 chief financial officers; (b) a national organization of local government technology leaders with 9,000 members; and (c) electronic government publication databases with the potential of reaching all 36,000 city, county, and township leaders. Unfortunately, the actual sample size was less than the target. A total of 68 responded to the survey, with 33 qualified participants completing the survey in its entirety. The low response rate may have been due to the time constraints or lack of interest that CIOs have in completing random surveys (Dues, 2010).

What could have been done differently? This is where a mixed method research study may have been more appropriate. Once the initial survey had been conducted, a suggestion would be to then focus on the database of respondents and conduct a qualitative study on the CIOs of these local governments. The intention would be to build specific case studies on how the variables correlated.

ACCURATELY MEASURING THE VARIABLES

Neuman (2006) defined internal validity as an assurance there are no errors internal to the design of the study, and that there are no alternative explanations for the way the dependent variables correlate to each other in the study. The common threats to internal validity include items such as selection bias, instrumentation errors, contamination, compensatory behavior, and experimenter expectancy. It is important that the possibility of any of the threats occurring in a study be extremely low. Selecting an independent survey firm to conduct the study is the first measure towards ensuring internal validity. Conducting an anonymous electronic survey ensures the participants of the study are randomly selected, their identities are not disclosed, and the survey results are coordinated and distributed without bias.

Neuman (2006) described external validity as the ability to generalize the findings from the study population sample to a broad range of individuals outside the study. Factors influencing external validity include realism and reactivity. Studies conducted through Internet surveys with a large population size from which to create a sample of unbiased participants, result in high external validity.

SURVEY INSTRUMENT

To be cognizant of the time constraints of the target population, the data collection tool must be easy to use and efficient to complete. A survey form is used to collect the data for the principal reason that the data is numeric and measurable (Salkind, 2003). The survey provides the opportunity to screen the participants and ensure the appropriate target population is being included. The survey should contain close-ended questions measured using a 5-point Likert scale. A custom survey may be needed in order to achieve adequate responses.

Potential participants must be advised that the survey is limited to individuals older than 18, with the qualifications identified in the study. The first screen of the survey should require the participant to affirm that the age and job position requirements are met. To proceed to the survey questions, participants are required to click on an "I Agree" button signifying these initial demographics are met. Advise participants that the data collected will be kept confidential, there will be no monetary gain from the study, and the data will be used strictly for research purposes.

In the Dues (2010) study, measures were taken to ensure the appropriateness of target population, anonymity, and time conscience. Introductory questions were used to confirm that the participants were senior technology leaders of local government organizations involved in implementing or supporting an ERP environment. As the survey questions filtered the respondents, respondents who had completed the survey but identified themselves as not being senior technology leaders of a public sector organization did not have their responses included in the analysis. There were other cases where respondents dropped out of the survey possibly because they did not meet the criteria for a senior technology leader.

Neuman (2006) equated reliability with dependability. If the sample population includes executives with significant job responsibilities and accountability, it is important that their anonymity be protected. By randomly inviting the study participants, and self-administering and electronically delivering the survey, confidentiality of the participants is maintained. The survey should not ask any personal questions. Names, addresses, or any other forms of identification of the participants should not be requested nor gathered in any manner during the survey process, with the exception of the participant's e-mail address if interested in receiving a copy of the survey results.

An independent Internet survey tool can be used to gather the data from the participants with no direct interaction with the researcher. As with all Internet transmissions, each participant's data submission includes a TCP/IP internetwork communications address specific to the participant's network or a particular host on that network. The survey service provider has access to the TCP/IP addresses of the participants, but the addresses are not forwarded to the researcher. Only the consolidated data responses are shared and used in the data analysis of the results.

In preparing the survey response choices, it is important to not underestimate the value of the option "Other". In the 2010 Dues study, there were a large number of "Other" ERP vendor responses. The "Other" results were analyzed separately in order to determine if there was any type of relationship among two of the variables. Because there was a high count of "Other" responses, as opposed to the selection of specified choices, an interesting turn in the study occurred. The participants in this category became a group that needed further exploration, suggesting the value of a qualitative case study.

DATA COLLECTION CHANNELS

The target sample size is used to identify channels for distributing the survey link to appropriate population. In the Dues (2010) study, the U.S. Census Bureau (2007) indicated a total of 36,011 municipalities, towns, and townships. To target as many of the public sector technology leaders as possible, the study is an example of using various technical channels to distribute the survey to the appropriate population. The study began with the intention of using only one survey distribution channel. A survey link was sent directly to a group of public sector city and county CIOs from the president of Metropolitan Information Exchange (MIX). This organization is comprised of chief information officers of cities and counties with populations over 100,000 (Metropolitan Information Exchange, 2010). The president of the organization posted an announcement of the research study survey to the membership of 58 individuals. A link to the survey website was included in the announcement. After the survey results were monitored, it became clear that too few responses were being received. Another point of survey distribution was needed.

Taking advantage of an affinity to technology, the thought was that senior technology leaders would participate in a survey posted on a popular industry-focused website. The Alliance for Innovation is an organization with 9,000 participating local governments that focus on new approaches to innovation in best practices for providing government services (Alliance for Innovation, 2010). The research study survey was posted to the member-only website with a request for participation from the membership. A link to the survey website was included in the blog. Once again, the survey response rate was low, which justified trying one more distribution channel.

To reach other public sector technology leaders advertising the survey link in multiple government publications was explored. The advertising was purchased "by-the-click." This provides the advertiser the ability to select publications and "bid" on advertising space. The higher the amount bid the more times the advertisement would pop up on the electronic publication. In the Dues (2010) Study advertising space was acquired in five different electronic publications: GCN—IT Management, GCN—State and Local, Internet .com—CIO, WT—State and Local, and Computerworld. Marchex Adhere was the company offering pay-per-click advertising on the publication websites (Marchex, 2010). Advertisements were posted on the publication websites requesting public sector technology leaders to complete the survey by accessing the survey link. Based on three diverse channels being used for the survey distribution, an adequate number of responses were received.

Survey responses were collected using the Internet data collection tool from SurveyMonkey (2010). A separate data collector was established for each channel: direct survey to MIX members, Internet blog at Alliance for Innovation website, and Marchex Internet marketing advertisement in the various government electronic publications. The collection processes were separated to ensure responses were received from each media channel. Further, this enabled monitoring the number of responses from each in the event the findings could be impacted. The survey website distributed the surveys and compiled the data. The results were downloaded to an Excel spreadsheet for additional data analysis.

FINDINGS

The research question was formulated to focus on the construct of interest, the leadership styles and type of ERP implemented by technology leaders of local governments with ERP sites perceived to be successful. In reviewing the data collected, there were no respondents that strongly disagreed with any of the questions, either on leadership style or perceived ERP success. A lack of response could be interpreted as a threat to validity. The participants may have been uncomfortable providing honest responses to questions that imply a role as leaders in an ERP environment is not successful. Another reason for low response rates could also have been that senior technology leaders are very busy, involved in high stress positions, and not apt to have an interest in taking the time to complete an online survey. If a mixed method study were used, the respondents could have been contacted to obtain more detailed information relative to their responses. Perhaps in a direct contact situation the participants would be more open and detailed with their success or failure supporting an ERP environment and the leadership skills needed in their role.

CONCLUSION

Quantitative research is an effective methodology to use for collecting data pertinent to specific variables. It is logical to assume that a large enough sample population can be assembled to ensure the results are significant in the field of study. However, if the population selected were one that may be hesitant to respond to surveys due to lack of time, lack of interest, or sensitivity of information, it would be better to proceed with a mixed study. Use the various survey distribution channels to obtain an adequate sample size. Take advantage of the various technology media available that will assist with survey distribution. Identifying an industry organization that can be contacted through the organization's website is a good option for reaching the appropriate population group. Posting a blog on an Internet publication can also bring attention to the survey. As a last resort, buying advertisement "by-the-click" can provide the ability to select publications read by individuals who are in the target population, and bring the survey to their attention. All three of these distribution channels could focus on the specific demographics of the target population.

Once the surveys have been conducted, follow-up interviews are recommended with a cross-section of the respondents. The interviews should be conducted with the intent to glean more information or details from the respondents in order to clarify the results. By combining quantitative and qualitative research methods, the results can be more thoroughly analyzed and presented with confidence.

REFERENCES

Aczel, A. D., & Sounderpandian, J. (2009). *Complete business statistics* (7th ed.). New York, NY: McGraw Hill.

Alliance for Innovation. (2010). *Alliance for innovation: Transforming local government.* Retrieved from http://transformgov.org/en/about/overview

Creswell, J. W. (2008). *Educational research: Planning, conducting, and evaluating quantitative and qualitative research* (2nd ed.). Upper Saddle River, NJ: Pearson Education, Inc.

Dues, P. M. (2010). Quantitative correlation of enterprise resource planning type, success and technology leadership style in local government. (Unpublished Doctoral dissertation). University of Phoenix, Phoenix, AZ.

Marchex. (2010). *Pay-per-click advertising.* Retrieved from http://www.marchex.com/pay-per-click-advertising

Metropolitan Information Exchange. (2010). *About MIX.* Retrieved from http://mixnet.org/

Neuman, W. L. (2006). *Social research methods: Qualitative and quantitative approaches* (6th ed.). Boston, MA: Allyn and Bacon.

Salkind, N. (2003). *Exploring research* (5th ed.). Upper Saddle River, NJ: Pearson Education, Inc.

SurveyMonkey (2010). *Everything you wanted to know but were afraid to ask.* Retrieved from http://www.surveymonkey.com/AboutUs.aspx

U.S. Census Bureau. (2007). *2007 census of governments.* Retrieved from http://www.census.gov/govs/cog/

About the Author

Dr. Patricia Dues is internationally known in the field of information technology. As an Information Technologies Manager for the City of Las Vegas, she has responsibility for the Enterprise Program Office and Applications Services.

A member of the board of directors of the Oracle Applications Users Group (OAUG) since 2001, Dr. Pat has served as president for three terms, among other executive offices. She chairs an international council as a member of the International Oracle Users Council (IOUC).

Dr. Pat holds accredited degrees that include: a Bachelor's Degree (BA) in Psychology from the University of Washington; a Masters of Business Administration (MBA) from University of Phoenix; and a Doctorate in Management in Organizational Leadership with a focus on Information Systems and Technology (DMIST) from the University of Phoenix, School of Advanced Studies. She received her Project Management Professional (PMP) certification in 2005.

Dr. Pat is currently an associate faculty member for University of Phoenix, Las Vegas and online campuses. She teaches in the School of Business and the Information Systems and Technology College.

Dr. Pat has been named the 2008 Las Vegas Emerging Public Administrator of the Year and Oracle Magazine 2009 User Group Evangelist.

To reach Dr. Patricia Dues for information on any of these topics, please email her at lvpat@aol.com

CHAPTER 9

New Paradigms for Research: Using Digital Tools for Mixed Methods Studies

Dr. Gail Ferreira

Change occurs because of paradigm shifts, which can lead to new theories (Kuhn, 1996). The inception of digital technologies has transformed the way that research is conducted today by providing multitudes of information in a home computing environment. The Internet has flattened and democratized information in a collaborative environment (Friedman, 2006). The ability to use these new capacities for research has become prevalent because of recent advances in technology.

Digital tools are being used for all phases of research projects, including idea inception, literature review, and data analysis, creating results and forming conclusions for the research. In this article, new paradigms for research will be explored and examined that can be used by doctoral learners to provide more substantive results.

IDEA INCEPTION

According to Collin and Porras (1994), Hewlett Packard founder David Packard understood that it is more important to know one is going as the world changes. Appreciative inquiry can be used for self-discovery and vision, using four processes that include (a) discover, (b) dream, (c) design, and (d) destiny (Cooperrider, Whitney, & Stavros, 2008).

One of the most important areas for when engaging in research is deciding on a topic, along with a proposed research methodology (qualitative, quantitative, or mixed-methods). Depending on your worldview, which is a blend of education, values, culture, and experience, a central research thesis is formed using different foci and perspectives (Combs, Bustamente, & Onwuegbuzie, 2010). Each researcher focuses on a problem using a unique perspective of these worldviews thereby creating a unique study regarding a central topic of interest.

While qualitative methodologies explore findings regarding a central problem (Creswell & Miller, 2000; Denzin & Lincoln, 2005), quantitative methodologies involve statistics, and use measurements to conclude about the states of objects (known as variables) that are being examined (Creswell & Plano Clark, 2007). Triangulation of methods provides the researcher with a greater degree of confidence in reporting findings, although subjective interpretation is still needed.

Using software tools for appreciative inquiry for mixed-methods research can help individuals understand themselves, and come up with new solutions using creative methods to expand upon ideas and preexisting knowledge. Tools such as MindMap software (MindMap, 2011) allow a researcher to start with a central topic and branch out into other thematic and sub-thematic ideas that evolve from the primary idea. Taken from the idea of a MindMap, which describes a note-taking technique that breaks away from traditional linear techniques, mind mapping software can be used to create models that can be used for all facets of research. Additionally, this technology tool can be used as an enabler to help visualize the central problem and purpose, translating the topic into themes that naturally evolve based on the worldviews of the researcher as illustrated in Figure 1 (Combs, Bustamente, & Onwuegbuzie, 2010).

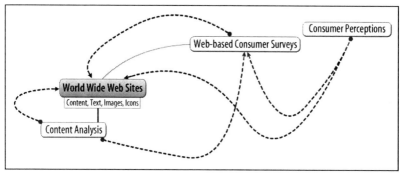

Figure 1. Using Mind Mapping software for research idea inception for mixed-methods research. From G. Ferreira (2007) "Perceptions of Consumers Regarding Global Web Sites".

LITERATURE REVIEW

The literature review is the crux of a research study, and reflects the values, goals, and direction of the research, using core methodologies to meld core tenets into a workable research design. The ability to use digital tools to help collect, organize, and visualize how research literature can be applied to the research study is valuable as a pictorial image of thematic development can help formulate research data collection and analysis methods.

Other tools, such as Web 2.0 using RSS Feeds, DIGG, DeLicious, and Twitter are a few ways to gather stores of information dynamically from research information stores such as university research libraries, or research Web sites such as Questia, Google Scholar, and other peer reviewed journal article and research book portals.

Web 2.0 Technologies. Web 2.0 technologies enable researchers to build a synergistic model for their research that uses the power of other collaborative research information stores to maximize their body of research knowledge. Using tools such as RSS Feeds (to save previously save research links in an Internet browser), DIGG (for saving research bookmarks), DeLicious (for saving research bookmarks), Twitter (to share research data, pictures, and video clips), and other Web 2.0 technologies for research, dynamic access to collective knowledge can be realized. Researchers can benefit by finding new techniques using Web 2.0 software to produce a high quality product in less time.

RSS Feeds. Using an RSS feed to save a previous search from is an excellent way to get dynamic updates from a research library regarding new publications related to your area of research interest. RSS stands for rich site summary, which is a way to distribute dynamically updated content over the Internet. RSS feeds are currently used by different types of commercial Web sites to provide up to date breaking information. One of the most common uses for an RSS feed is by a network news site (for example http://www .cnn.com, http://www.foxnews.com) to display latest breaking news and announcements. For research, you can use RSS feeds to automatically collect new peer reviewed journal articles on topics of interest. You can embed the ability to use an RSS feed by embedding the functionality into an Internet browser toolbar, or you can use the built in functionality provided by the research library portal.

RSS feeds are excellent tool to streamline research using the research library, to save previous information retrieved from a query. Additionally, RSS feeds can be used to provide continual updates to content from other literary Web sites, including books, magazines, journal sites, and publishers.

Once you create an RSS feed, it creates a URL in a pop-up window for your reference. This URL will be available to you from the left side of your Internet browser and dynamically update as new content is added to your search. This accomplishes two things: (a) it will save you time by saving a previously constructed search, and (b) it will dynamically update the results of the query with newly added material, ensuring that your research is current.

DIGG. DIGG is a social networking site that relies on information that comes directly from members of the community. Registered users submit DIGG-worthy content which includes news stories, blog entries, videos, and pictures to the site by writing and linking back to the piece. Then other members of the registered user community rank the document with Diggs or votes on the article, and the highest ranks are posted on the DIGG Web site. Submitted articles are ranked in popularity by the number of DIGGs they get by users selecting a DIGG icon by using an embedded DIGG toolbar. Although DIGG is not a traditional source for peer reviewed journal articles, there are ways to find information from relevant trade journals, newspapers, and other relevant sources by conducting a category search by selecting a specific topic from the drop down menu. For example, choosing the category title World & Business -> Business & Finance which yields the top ranked articles from the user community of interest. From this list of articles, you can start your research by finding relevant topics in business that is not only timely, but extremely relevant to business.

Additionally, you can use DIGG to push out information to a Web site that is relevant to the community. First of all, to you need to embed DIGG in an Internet browser such as Firefox by clicking on the install Toolbar option on Firefox. The DIGG Toolbar for Firefox lets you DIGG, submit content, and keep track of DIGG even when you're not on the DIGG site itself. With a notification window built into the toolbar, you'll never miss a popular story or when friends DIGG, submit, or comment on stories. Once you run the program, you have an embedded icon that you can use to tag any articles that you find interesting in your research DIGG not only is a great site to gauge the pulse of topics, but also a way to contribute to the world of knowledge. Blogs, scholarly articles, or other relevant content can be published onto the DIGG site using the following steps: (a) publish an article on your blog, (b) create an account on DIGG, (c) go to the submit a story page on DIGG,

(d) follow the instructions, (e) note the URL of your story on DIGG (i.e., http://www.digg.com/your-category/the-title-you-gave-it), (f) edit your post and add a caption to the bottom of the article: Like this article? [a href=www.digg.com/your-category/the-title-you-gave-it]Digg it[/a]! If your article manages to get 500+ DIGGS, you will see a serious jump in your Web traffic.

DeLicious. DeLicious is a Web site (http://www.delicious.com) that acts as social bookmarking service, which means you can save and share all your bookmarks online, tag and organize them to make your research more efficient. Additionally, you can obtain bookmarks from the other users by performing a general keyword search. Similar to the other social networking sites, you can embed a toolbar icon in your browser that will mark a specific article for inclusion into your set of tags, which act as a dynamic way for you to organize information based on your interest. After logging into DeLicious (http://www.delicious.com) with a user account, you first perform a general search on a topic of interest. Once you find specific articles, you mark and tag them, which build a hierarchical directory of tags that you can use as your own personal workspace to organize and rank your results.

Twitter. Twitter is a social networking site (http://www.twitter .com) where users share information by giving status updates. The best way to use Twitter is from your cell phone, where you can provide dynamic updates while you are in transit or articles known as Tweets. These updates can include attachments such as text, pictures, and any other file that you can attach to a mobile phone. Twitter uses two primary categories: followers, and following. You can select followers by performing keyword searches on people, topic, or places. From that search, a list of people will appear that you can select and follow based on your interest level. Alternatively, others can choose you based on their interests and meaningful keyword searches for specific terms, which gets tallied in your following. Although Twitter is a powerful marketing tool, it can also be used for research because of its versatility and dynamic search abilities. In Twitters navigation search bar, Twitter Search has the ability to search for key words, locations, phrases, and more. You can gauge the pulse of the market by asking questions regarding what people think, commonly used phrases, company keyword searches and more. Twitter also supports multiple language translations, by translating foreign languages tweets into English. Additionally, you can filter by language; perform keyword tracking, and lots of meaningful search results, known as trending traffic.

This technology could be useful to a single or group research project by providing a mechanism to send and receive messages from following or followers, who could be asked a series of questions sent as Tweets over an iPhone or other device, and provide a meaningful response back along with pictures, text, and other documents that could prove as useful information to use in a mixed-methods research study as exploratory documentation. Alternatively, it could be used to pull meaningful content that has already been posted using meaningful keyword searches.

RESEARCH METHODOLOGY

Digital software tools can be used for all facets of the research methodology, including the collection of data, the dissemination of results, and variable measurement. Qualitative research is used to explore phenomena, using questions that are prefaced with what, how, or why in order to gain experiential information based on the lived experiences of the participants (Creswell, 2003; Denzin & Lincoln, 2005; Moustakas, 1994, Patton, 2004). With roots in nursing research, qualitative research allows the researcher to gain knowledge by the ability to interview the participant using verbal and nonverbal cues (Moustakas, 1994; Patton, 2004). While quantitative research starts with a hypothesis, and proves the hypothesis through the study, qualitative research finds new principles based on the method chosen to collect data (Creswell, 2003).

DATA COLLECTION

Qualitative interviews. The ability to probe individuals by conducting qualitative interviews allows the researcher to uncover new thematic elements that provides unexpected findings, while quantitative studies only prove or disprove the hypotheses based on data. The qualitative research interview seeks to describe and the meanings of central themes in the life world of the subjects. The main task in interviewing is to understand the meaning of what the interviewees say (Kvale, 1996). A qualitative research interview seeks to cover both a factual and a meaning level, though it is usually more difficult to interview on a meaning level. (Kvale, 1996). Interviews are particularly useful for getting the story behind a participant's experiences. The interviewer can pursue in-depth information around the topic to gain my insight and depth. Interviews may be useful as follow-up to certain respondents to questionnaires, e.g., to further investigate their responses (Patton, 2004). The number of participants in a qualitative interview are less than in a quantitative survey; with the average falling between 10–20 participants, and thematic analysis is finalized after saturation is reached with the exploration of data (Creswell, 2003; Patton, 2004).

Quantitative surveys. Quantitative research methods and surveys are associated with the examination of the relationship between and among variables are central to answering questions and hypotheses through surveys and experiments (Creswell, 2003). A survey design provides a quantitative or numeric description of trends, attitudes, or opinions of a population by studying a sample of that population. Consequently, from sample research, the researcher generalizes or makes claims of knowledge about the population. In addition, the fundamental components of the survey design is the purpose of the survey research, the population and sample, the instrumentation, the variables in the study, and the data analysis (Creswell, 2007; Creswell & Clark, 2007).

Calculating participants. The number of participants for a quantitative study needs a power analysis in order to come up with an optimal result. Shareware software such as G*Power (Erdfelder, Faul, & Buchner, 1996) can be used to determine how many participants are needed for a quantitative study. The theoretical underpinnings of Power Analysis provides methods for calculating the minimum effect size likely to be detected in the quantitative experiment given sample size, in addition to the standard methods of calculating minimum sample size required to accept a statistical test given a specific level of confidence (Trochim & Donnelly, 2008). Setting variables including the acceptable level of power, an alpha significance value, and a medium level effect size based on similar studies, an acceptable size for participants can be calculated and used for the research.

Digital data collection. The use of internet data collection tools such as SurveyMonkey has become prevalent as a way to distribute and manage the data collection process (SurveyMonkey, 2011). The use of email distribution lists to send out all correspondence regarding the data collection, including the link to the questionnaire, has become a popular method to collect data. After the data is collected, the user can upload the results into software or reporting tools to complete the data analysis process.

DATA ANALYSIS

Qualitative research. Data analysis can be conducted using qualitative research methods, coupled with digital software techniques. The researcher can begin their study by importing all of the data from the interview into the software such as NVivo (QSR International, 2011), and place the items in a structured folder system on a computer. Next, interconnections of data, called pattern theories (Guba & Lincoln, 1985), can be discovered by setting up themes regarding common elements in the study. Multiple sources of data can be collected and analyzed from the survey content to ensure validity of the research findings (Creswell, 2007; Shadish, Cook, & Campbell, 2002). The data elements gathered came from data sources imported into the NVivo software from the survey results and combined with any other addendums or notes to create thematic elements that are used to build the results and conclusions for a research study.

Quantitative research. Quantitative methods are associated with the way of thinking and examining issues rationally. Hence, they are not only important for all kinds of research, but also for everyday living (Bryman & Bell, 2007). Quantitative research methods are a way of making knowledge claims by determining what true knowledge is and what constitutes acceptable evidence. In addition, they are a way of employing appropriate questionnaire surveys of discovering or verifying knowledge and analyzing data. Creswell (2003) and Zikmund (2003) indicate that while quantitative research methods have been available for decades, but it still developing in form and substance. Consequently, quantitative research is the systematic scientific investigation of quantitative properties and phenomena and their relationships. The objective of quantitative research is to develop and employ mathematical models, theories and/or hypotheses pertaining to natural phenomena. The process of measurement is central to quantitative research because it provides the fundamental connection between empirical observation and mathematical expression of quantitative relationships (Schmidt & Hollensen, 2006).

SPSS is the statistical software that is primarily used for the analysis of data in quantitative studies (IBM, 2011). The aim of quantitative research is to find the relationship, if any, between the independent and dependent variable(s), and software such as SPSS allows the researcher to upload the interview data and analyze the results. Although correlational research is limited in practical application because the proof of correlation does not imply causation (Zikmund, 2003), the ability to uncover the results using software helps manage large stores of data, as quantitative research uses hundreds of participants.

Other tools. Many research studies use inanimate objects such as computers as participants, enabling the use of unique digital tools for data analysis. For the software industry, studies have been conducted using computers as participants, and testing software such as NCover complete for data analysis (Nakkhongkham, 2011). Another study using quantitative, experimental research design to study statistical demand forecasting using MapReduce programs in a cloud computing environment was used for quantitative research (Sandholm, 2008; Sullivan, 2011). Other research studies by Abdulhadi (2008), Sandholm (2008), and Tintamuski acted as precedents to experimental research using computers as participants, and software to measure the relationships, if any, between the independent variable and the dependent variable.

CONCLUSION

The ability to think out of the box and to apply research principles using digital tools has helped produce novel research studies, enabling the researcher to come up with results and conclusions that were previously not possible using manual tools. Not only are digital tools a timesaver, but they can process large amounts of information efficiently, providing rich results that are accurate and conclusive for research. As the methods and techniques continue to evolve, researchers will continue to produce research studies that use these techniques in an increasingly efficient fashion. The ability to effectively collaborate with other researchers will also become more enhanced with social networking tools and blogs that can allow researchers to find others with the same interests and be able to share their research results electronically via use of these new mediums. Manuscripts, data, models, and other assets can be stored and reused or modified for further research and analysis. As the evolution for these tools continues, so will the development of new research tools and more precise applications of methodology, with the exploration and examination of topics becoming more sophisticated and precise. The discovery of new theories should become more probable as researchers dream and innovate new ideas, unleashing the power of digital tools.

REFERENCES

Abdulhadi, A. (2008). *Examining the impact of nested web services on response time.*

Bryman, A., & Bell, E. (2007). *Business research methods* (2nd ed.). Oxford, England: University Press.

Collins, J., & Porras, J. I. (1994). *Built to last: Successful habits of visionary companies.* New York, NY: HarperCollins.

Combs, J. P., Bustamante, R. M., & Onwuegbuzie, A. J. (2010). An interactive model for facilitating development of literature reviews. *International Journal of Multiple Research Approaches,* 4(2), 159–182. doi: 10.5172/mra.2010.4.2.159

Cooperrider, D., Whitney, D., & Stavros, J. M. (2008). *Appreciative Inquiry Handbook: For leaders of change.* Brunswick, OH: Crown Custom Publishing. Walnut Creek, CA: Berrett-Koehler Publishers.

Creswell, J. W., & Miller, D. L. (2000). Determining validity in qualitative inquiry. *Theory into Practice, 39*(3), 124–131.

Creswell, J.W. (2003). Research design: *Qualitative, quantitative, and mixed methods approaches. (2nd ed.).* Thousand Oaks, CA: Sage Publications.

Creswell, J. W., & Plano Clark V. L. (2007). *Designing and conducting mixed methods research.* Thousand Oaks, CA: Sage Publications.

Denzin, N. K., & Lincoln, Y. S. (2005). *The Sage handbook of qualitative research* (3rd ed.). Thousand Oaks, CA: Sage Publications.

Erdfelder, E., Faul, F., & Buchner, A. (1996). *G*Power* (Version 3.1) [Computer software]. Retrieved from http://www.psycho.uni-duesseldorf.de/aap/projects/gpower/

Ferreira, G. (2007). Consumer perceptions of global branding and iconization. (Doctoral dissertation). Retrieved from Dissertations & Theses. (Publication No. AAT 3272246)

Giorgi, A. (1985). *Phenomenology and psychological research.* Pittsburgh, PA: Duquesne University.

Guba, E. G., & Lincoln, Y. S. (1994). *Handbook of qualitative research.* Thousand Oaks, CA: Sage Publications.

IBM. (2011). *IBM Home Page.* Retrieved from http://www.ibm.com

Kuhn, T. S. (1996). *The structure of scientific revolutions. (3rd ed.).* Chicago, IL: University of Chicago Press.

Kvale, S. (1996). *InterViews: An introduction to qualitative research interviewing.* Thousand Oaks, CA: Sage Publications.

Leedy, P. D., & Ormrod, J. E. (2005). *Practical research: Planning and design* (8th ed.).Upper Saddle River, NJ: Prentice Hall.

Miller, D. C., & Salkind, N.J. (2002). *Handbook of research design and social measurement* (6th ed.). Chapter 4.8, pp. 162–164. Thousand Oaks, CA: Sage.

MindMap. (2011). *MindMap Home Page.* Retrieved from http://www.mindmap.com

Moustakas, C. (1994). *Phenomenological research methods.* Thousand Oaks, CA: Sage Publications.

Nakkhongham, S. (2011). Assessing the relationship between prerelease software testing and product defects discovered. (Unpublished dissertation). Northcentral University, Prescott AZ.

Patton, M. Q. (2004). *Qualitative research & evaluative methods.* London, UK: Sage Publications.

QSR International. (2006). *QSR home page.* Retrieved from http://www.qsrinternational.com

Sandholm, T., & Lai, K. (2009). *MapReduce optimization using regulated dynamic prioritization.* Seattle, WA: SIGMETRICS/Performance.

Schmidt, M. J., & Hollensen, S. (2006). *Marketing research: An international approach.* UK: Prentice Hall.

Shadish, W. R., Cook, T. D., & Campbell, D. T. (2002). *Experimental and quasiexperimental designs for generalized causal inference.* Boston, MA: Houghton-Mifflin.

Sullivan, J. (2011). *Assessing the impact of MapReduce program design on Response Time.* (Unpublished doctoral dissertation). Northcentral University, Prescott AZ.

SurveyMonkey. (2011). *Home page.* Retrieved from http://www.surveymonkey.com/

Tintamuski, Y. (2010). *Examining the relationship between organization systems and information security awareness.* Trochim, W., & Donnelly, J. (2008). *The research methods knowledge base.* Mason, OH: Cengage Learning.

Vogt, W. P. (2006). *Quantitative research methods for professionals in education and other fields.* Boston, MA: Pearson Education, Inc.

Zikmund, W. G. (2003). *Business research methods.* Mason, OH: Thomson Learning.

About the Author

Dr. Gail Ferreira holds several accredited degrees: a Bachelor of Science (BS) in Computer Science from National University; a Master of Science (MS) in Computer Science from National University; and a Doctor of Management (DM) from University of Phoenix.

Dr. Ferreira is an educational and research technical expert who actively teaches for both industry and academia. She teaches and develops educational materials for a breadth of research, writing, and technical courses at an advanced level, having taught thousands of students in the last 5 years in both an online as well as a live learning environment.

In academia, she works with Walden University as an Associate Professor for the Doctorate of Business Administration program; and Northcentral University where she is the Applied Computing Science Lead, setting the pace for Northcentral Universities' Doctoral level course design and development. Dr. Gail is also on faculty with Strayer University, University of the Rockies, and University of Phoenix. Additionally, she acts as a committee chairperson for doctoral dissertation research, specializing in qualitative, quantitative, and mixed methodologies.

Dr. Gail is an independent technical solutions consultant and project manager, with expertise with enterprise software solutions including Vignette, Kronos, and Oracle.

To reach Dr. Gail Ferreira for information on any of these topics, please email: drgail.ferreira@gmail.com

CHAPTER 10

A Quantitative Exploration of Team Effectiveness

Dr. Rachel A. Gonzales

This chapter is a summation of the 2010 Gonzales Study on health care team effectiveness. The chapter begins with an overview of the research problem and introduction to the three variables of the study. An emphasis on the methodology and results is provided, followed by a general discussion of the study's findings. The two remaining sections: (a) recommendations, and (b) limitations and future research directions, provide opportunities for future scholarly works. The research scholar can use this chapter to frame ideas for future research or formulation of an appropriate methodology for his or her own research.

BACKGROUND

Throughout the centuries, groups in organizations have transformed into complex entities called teams (Kozlowski & Ilgen, 2006). The term *groups* as applied in the 2010 Gonzales Study referred to individuals working together; whereas, teams referred to individuals working together for a common purpose (Katzenbach & Smith, 1993; Saltman, O'Dea, Farmer, Veitch, Rosen, & Kidd, 2007). Teamwork is a current organizational solution to the complexity of tasks and processes that is a constant in contemporary health care institutions (Delgado-Pina, Romero-Martinez, & Gomez-

Martinez, 2008). As documented by the literature, a problem or recurring poor teamwork exists in the health care industry (Kavanaugh & Cowan, 2004; Takase, Maude, & Manias, 2005). To reduce teaming issues, costs, and improve the quality and safety of patient care, health care leaders require information that contributes to team effectiveness (American Hospital Association, 2007).

Team effectiveness is multi-dimensional, with many complex components required for a team to function well (Kang, Yang, & Rowley, 2006). Limited studies correlate team effectiveness with psychosocial team attributes, such as emotional competence or norms (Elfenbein, 2006; Leggat, 2007). The 2010 Gonzales Study identified the relationship among the previously mentioned factors through research into the affiliation among *team task interdependence* (a team process); *group emotional competence;* (a psychosocial attribute); and *team effectiveness.*

TEAM TASK INTERDEPENDENCE

Teams exhibit interdependencies in workflow, goals, and outcomes (Hollenbeck et al., 1995). Recognition of team interdependence began with Thompson (1967), who focused on team interdependence, and the role within an organization. Shea and Guzzo (1987) added to the theoretical framework of task interdependence through approaching the construct from a structural-behavioral framework. Building on task interdependence as a structural-behavioral framework, Johnson and Johnson (1989) viewed task interdependence as an accountability factor of team members and their respective roles within the team. Wageman (1995) complemented the team task interdependence construct by defining team task interdependence as "the degree a task requires collective action" (p. 146) through the sharing of resources.

Multiple studies have identified the importance of team task and the relationship of team task to team effectiveness (Hsu, Wang,

Chen, & Yu, 2007; Tata & Prasad, 2004). According to the research, low team interdependence equates to team members functioning as individuals (Katz-Navon, 2005). Conversely, high task interdependence is associated with higher team member communication and support (Gundlach, Zivnuska, & Stoner, 2006). When team interdependence is high, group members are more likely to function as a team (Gully, Incalcaterra, Joshi, & Beaubien, 2002).

GROUP EMOTIONAL COMPETENCE

Salovey and Mayer (1990) defined emotional intelligence as "the subset of social intelligence that involves the ability to monitor one's own and others feelings and emotions, to discriminate among them and to use . . . information to guide one's thinking and actions" (p. 189). Building upon this theoretical framework, Amundson (2003) explored the influence of individual emotional intelligence and group emotional competence. Cherniss (2001) identified a distinction, stating that a team comprised of individuals who possess a high emotional intelligence is not equivalent to group emotional competence.

The study of team emotional intelligence is occurring through team norms (Amundson, 2003; Gantt & Agazarian, 2004; Stubbs, 2005). Druskat and Wolff (2001b) defined group emotional competence as "the ability of a group to generate a shared set of norms that manage the emotional process in a way that builds trust, group identity, and group efficacy" (p. 138). Wolff, Druskat, Koman, and Messer (2006) later drew a positive relationship between group emotional competence and group effectiveness. Druskat and Wolff (2001b) measured group emotional competence in the terms of emotionally competent group norms.

Emotional group competence norms, or *norms,* are rules and expectations within the group emotional structure, which have beneficial emotional consequences through their positive influence on the development of group emotional competence (Wolff, Druskat, Koman, & Messer, 2006). Emotional behavior norms are the core of group emotional competence theory (Cherniss, 2001). Wolff, Druskat, Koman, and Messer (2006) asserted team outcomes are determined by the norms or patterns of interactions. According to Wolff et al. (2006), current research fails to address the role team norms have with team tasks. Goleman, Boyatzis, and McKee (2002) stated discovering a team's emotional reality can heighten a team's effectiveness.

EFFECTIVE TEAMWORK

Amundson's (2003) research on group emotional competence and team effectiveness provided a baseline for the 2010 Gonzales Study. This research complements Amundson's (2003) research by focusing on the relationship team task interdependence, with group emotional competence, as a prediction factor in team effectiveness. Many definitions, measures, and models of team effectiveness are documented in the literature (Cantu, 2007). McShane and Von Glinow (2005) provided a clear, concise, and theoretically based definition of team effectiveness: "the extent to which a team achieves its objectives, achieves the needs and objectives of its members, and sustains itself—over time" (p. 271). Effective teams have emotional intelligence, which is specifically demonstrated in technical, social, and interactional skills (McCallin & Bamford, 2007). Teamwork increases or decreases, depending on how well individuals work together (McCallin & Bamford, 2007).

METHOD

The purpose of the 2010 Gonzales Study was to apply quantitative, correlational research to examine if relationships existed among team task interdependence, group emotional competence, and the effectiveness of teams in hospitals. A quantitative method enabled the analysis of research with a large quantity of data (Creswell, 2005). Furthermore, a correlational research design provided an opportunity to explore a possible relationship of the study's variables. The two interrogative questions that guided the study were: (1) what is the predictive ability of team task interdependence and group emotional competence, independently, in team effectiveness; and (2) what interaction, if any, is present between team task interdependence and group emotional competence, and if so, how does the interaction affect team effectiveness.

The 2010 Gonzales Study incorporated analysis of the variables found in a survey of 83 health care teams, of four acute care hospitals. Teams in the study complied with the following definition of a team: A group of three or more people, with complementary abilities and skills and committed to a common purpose (Hollenbeck, Ilgen, Sego, Hedlund, Major, & Phillips, 1995; Katzenbach & Smith, 1993). Various types of health care teams were used; teams were not restricted to one type of discipline or role in the organization, to help eliminate potential discrepancies.

Collection of data occurred primarily through use of previously validated instruments: Liden, Wayne, and Bradway (1997) team task interdependence scale (TTI), Druskat and Wolff's (2006) group emotional competence survey (GEC), and Amundson's (2003) team effectiveness scale (TES). The intended purpose of the TTI was to measure the level of team member's task interdependence (Liden, Wayne, & Bradway, 1997). The GEC was comprised of 57 questions, representing nine team norms (Wolff, 2006). Each of the nine team norms was comprised of five to eight questions (Koman & Wolff, 2008). Amundson's (2003) TES consisted of seven effectiveness determinants as perceived by the internal team members.

Data collection process began with the distribution of the survey packets to the hospital site leader who agreed to facilitate the survey collection. Follow-up phone calls and e-mails to coordinate the administration of the surveys occurred immediately after the receipt of the survey packets and throughout the survey administration period. Survey administration occurred over 6 weeks. An assumption made was the majority of the teams within the organization met at least once during the data collection period. Survey packets included: (a) an introductory letter to the leader; (b) survey instructions for the team lead and the team member; (c) informed consent; (d) surveys; and (e) a postage pre-paid return package. The survey packets were organized and pre-labeled with the appropriate team identification. For example, Hospital A had 35 teams. Each of the 35 teams had an individual team survey packet. All of the team packets included enough surveys for every team member, labeled with the team's particular identification, such as A-MST for a medical surgical team within hospital A. The process of team identification enabled clear identification of each team and the participation from each team.

The 2010 Gonzales Study applied the following scoring system for each instrument: (a) TES is a sum of the seven items, with reverse scoring used with all items (referred to as Team TES Sum); (b) TTI is a sum the three items (referred to as Team TTI Sum); and (c) GEC is a mean across all of the subscales (referred to as Team GEC Mean). The team effectiveness scale had strong reliability with $\alpha = .92$. The lowest alpha statistic was seen for the team task interdependence scale $\alpha = .75$. The subscales of the group emotional competence survey all had good reliability, ranging from $\alpha = .80$ for GEC SelfEval to $\alpha = .92$ for GEC SelfRegulate.

RESULTS

Eighty-three teams comprised of 499 individual team members, from four hospitals, responded to the surveys documented in the 2010 Gonzales Study. Hospital A represented the greatest number of team participation, with 34 teams, and 188 individual team members. Hospital C represented the smallest portion of the sample, with eight teams, consisting of 53 individual team members. The delineation of team type was rated by team members' perception of whether the team was primarily clinical or non-clinical. A majority of the teams were identified as clinical, 42 teams, representing 50.6% of the sample. Team size was the second adjustment variable analyzed for the purposes of the study. The majority of the teams, 28, or 33.73%, consisted of six to nine team members.

Analysis of variance (ANOVA) was used to determine if average team effectiveness differed between hospitals or by team type or size. Further analysis of the adjustment variable, team type and size, through the calculation of means by team type and size, demonstrated there were no significant differences in team means. Team GEC Mean approached significance with p = 0.057. A lack of statistical significance with team means by team size supports team size is not a moderating variable of team task interdependence or team effectiveness.

The analysis of the adjustment variable of hospital distribution demonstrated a significant difference for Team TES Sum and Team GEC Mean based on which hospital a team was associated. Team effectiveness and group emotional competence demonstrated a variance among hospitals. Lowest scores of GEC Mean and TES SUM were consistently seen at hospital C. Highest scores for GEC Mean and TES SUM were consistently at hospital A. Team TTI Sum was not significant based on means by hospital distribution. Team task interdependence did not show the same level of variance among hospitals as team effectiveness and group emotional competence, a result that suggested a consistency among hospitals with high task interdependent teams.

RESEARCH QUESTION ONE

Two interrogative questions were applied in the 2010 Gonzales

Study. The first question was, what is the predictive ability of team task interdependence and group emotional competence, independently, in team effectiveness? Investigation of question one subsequently occurred through the use of Pearson correlations. This research question drove the testing of two null hypotheses.

H1. The level of team task interdependence does not predict team effectiveness. The null hypothesis was rejected as team task interdependence and team effectiveness were significantly correlated with a Pearson correlation coefficient of .576 ($p < .001$). Rejection of the null hypothesis supports the assertion that team task interdependence is a predictor of team effectiveness.

A primary perception of the team members within the study was that the teams individuals served on are highly task interdependent, as represented with a mean Team TTI Sum of 17.11. As previously asserted, the 2010 Gonzales Study demonstrated that team effectiveness is essential for health care teams. Staples and Webster (2008) argued as the task interdependencies of a team increase, the need for team effectiveness increases. Results of the data analysis surrounding H1 demonstrated a statistically significant positive relationship between team task interdependence and team effectiveness. The higher the team task interdependence is of a team, the higher degree of team effectiveness. Health care teams have high degree team interdependence, much more than other industries and consistent with the findings of the study (Nembhard & Edmondson, 2006).

H2. The level of group emotional competence documented in the 2010 study did not not predict team effectiveness. The null hypothesis was rejected because group emotional competence and team effectiveness were significantly correlated with a Pearson correlation coefficient of .865 ($p < .001$). Rejection of the null hypothesis supported the assertion that group emotional competence is a predictor of team effectiveness.

A linear regression model was developed to test if both the GEC and TTI predicted Team TES independently. In the first model (refer to Gonzales 2010), the main effects of team task interdependence and group emotional competence was investigated. In the first iteration, each GEC subscale and the overall GEC mean were available to enter the model in stepwise fashion; only the overall GEC mean entered, so the subscales were not included in any subsequent models. The adjusted R2 for model one was .75, indicating that about 75% of the variability in team effectiveness score is explained by team task interdependence and group emotional competence. Both predictors were significant. Group emotional competence was the much stronger predictor, with a t-statistic of 11.99 and a p-value < .001. Consistent with the Pearson correlation results reported in above. Team task interdependence and group emotional competence, independently, demonstrate a predictive relationship with team effectiveness. Group emotional competence was identified to be a stronger predictor of the two, suggesting the level of group emotional competence would provide the greater leverage for enhancing team effectiveness.

The supporting statistical results presented in the 2010 study demonstrated a positive relationship with group emotional competence and team effectiveness is significant in providing further validation of group emotional intelligence theory. Amundson (2003) and Stubbs (2005) found that group emotional competence was related to team effectiveness, affirming a consistency with the present study's findings. The 2010 Gonzales Study further validated Koman and Wolff's (2001b) theory and supported the conclusion that the higher the group emotional competence of a team, the higher the level of team effectiveness.

RESEARCH QUESTION TWO

The second question examined what interaction, if any, is present between team task interdependence and group emotional competence, and if so, how does the interaction affect team effectiveness? The null hypothesis (H3) associated with research question two was: Team task interdependence and group emotional competence do not interact. The third null hypothesis was rejected, supporting the assertion that team task interdependence and group emotional competence have a positive interaction that affects team effectiveness.

Research question two was investigated by creating an interaction term between group emotional competence and team task interdependence. The term was added to the model, to identify whether the effects of team task interdependence and group emotional competence on effectiveness were independent of each other, or if the level of one affected the effect of the other. Results of model 2 indicated that the interaction term is a significant moderating variable (refer to Gonzales 2010). The adjusted R2 for model two was .759. That is, the effect of team task interdependence and group emotional competence are not entirely independent; the effect of both together is slightly less than the sum of each independently. The 2010 Gonzales Study concluded that group emotional competence and team task interdependence taken together have a greater ability of positively influencing team effectiveness than the factors do separately.

TEAM EFFECTIVENESS MODEL

Health care leaders do not achieve results alone; leaders require effective teams to achieve performance objectives (Kaiser, Hogan, & Craig, 2008). Leaders can influence and create effective team environments (Kaiser, et al., 2008). A team effectiveness model was an outgrowth of the 2010 research (see Figure 1). The model is a combination of the results of the Gonzales (2010) research applied to McShane and Von Glinow's (2005) team effectiveness model. The model represents the positive relationship of team task interdependence as a type of team design on team effectiveness, and group emotional competence, defined as team norms having a positive relationship with team effectiveness.

The 2010 Gonzales Study used McShane and Von Glinow's (2005) model of team effectiveness as a theoretical basis. McShane and Von Glinow's model consists of the following core components: (a) organizational and team environment, (b) team design, and (c) team processes. Gonzales (2010) measured the constructs of team design and team process, including team effectiveness.

According to McShane and Von Glinow (2005), three potential variables are associated with *team design*. McShane and Von Glinow (2005) proposed task characteristics, team size, and team composition as the three potential characteristics of team design. Instruments of the Gonzales (2010) study collected data on each of the three variables. The research identified team size and team composition as adjustment variables, and no statistical significance was seen in relationship to team effectiveness. Task characteristic was measured through the construct of team task interdependence. The 2010 study identified a significant relationship between team task interdependence and team effectiveness, providing support of the team effectiveness model of McShane and Von Glinow (2005).

Multiple potential variables associated with *team process* exist. McShane and Von Glinow (2005) identified task development, team norms, team roles, and team cohesion as potential characteristics of team process. The present research provided data regarding team norms as defined by Druskat and Wolff (1999) through the construct of group emotional competence. Further, Druskat and Wolff concluded that group emotional competence demonstrated a strong predictive relationship with team effectiveness, providing additional scholarly support for the McShane and Von Glinow (2005) model.

McShane and Von Glinow's (2005) model demonstrated relationships between team design and team effectiveness as well as between team process and team effectiveness. The proposed team effectiveness model demonstrates a merger of the constructs and findings of the 2010 study with McShane and Von Glinow (2005) model (see Figure 1). Two primary constructs define the team effectiveness model: (1) Team task interdependence as a type of team design positively affects team effectiveness; and (2) Group emotional competence as a team process through team norms has a positive relationship with team effectiveness.

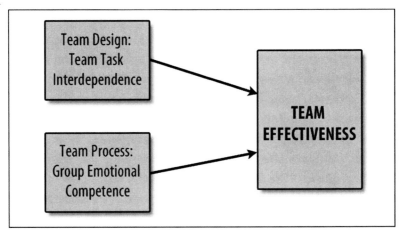

Figure 1. Team Effectiveness Model.

RECOMMENDATIONS

The following recommendations provided by Gonzales (2010) serve as a mechanism for building team effectiveness among key stakeholders, such as team and organizational leaders. Effective teamwork is a viable organizational solution to the complexity of issues facing institutions (Delgado-Pina et al., 2008). Teams should be intentionally structured to enhance task interdependence; Gonzales (2010) concluded that team task interdependence is positively correlated to team effectiveness. The design of a team can affect task interdependence (Hertel, Konradt, & Orlikowski, 2004). Leaders are responsible for the design of teams and have the control to establish, respect, and foster task interdependence, thereby enhancing teamwork (DeRue & Morgenson, 2007). Teams can be established while considering the level of task interdependence of the team. Health care leaders focusing on efficiency and efficacy often reconsider the structures of a team, the members of team. Redesign of team structures should include maintaining or enhancing the task interdependence of the team.

The 2010 Gonzales Study concluded it is necessary to foster and support group emotional competence constructs through education of team norms. The theoretical basis for the recommendation was substantiated through the newness of group emotional competence as a team effectiveness construct (Zeidner, Roberts, & Matthews, 2004). Education can occur through the basis of team norms as outlined by Wolff (2006). High group emotional competence can have a positive effect on team effectiveness (Stubbs, 2005). Ultimately, the 2010 Gonzales Study concluded that concerted education of groups to develop emotional competence through team norms could enhance team effectiveness.

Six dimensions of group emotional competence exist: (a) team awareness of members, (b) team regulation of members, (c) team self-awareness, (d) team self-regulation, (e) team social awareness, and (f) team social skills (Wolff, 2006). Each dimension included team norms. Other health care leaders can perform team assessments and determine the deficient team norms as they are the fundamental topics for education (Gonzales, 2010). For example, the dimension of *team self regulation* can be enhanced through the team setting ground rules and using the rules to point out errant behaviors (Druskat & Wolff, 2001a). The 2010 Gonzales Study provide the basis for the assertion that health care leaders can teach teams to become more emotionally competent groups and enhance the efficacy of the team.

LIMITATIONS AND FUTURE RESEARCH DIRECTIONS

Multiple moderating variables of team effectiveness exist, such as time, team orientation, empowerment, process, and interdependence (Bunderson, 2003; Mathieu, Maynard, Rapp, & Gilson, 2008). The 2010 Gonzales Study omitted three variables: time, power, and team orientation. The researcher concluded these variables should be recognized as a limitation and considered in future research. The 2010 study recognized the potential contributing factors of three adjustment variables- team type, team size, and hospital distribution, which were subsequently collected and analyzed. Potential moderating variables not explored in the 2010 Gonzales study could warrant further exploration to identify prospective relationships with team effectiveness.

Social science research constructs can be challenging to measure (Hall, 2008). Many teams lack objective performance measures, leading to the rationale of why a majority of the tools measuring team effectiveness are through team perception (Afarjanc, Serapinas, & Daugviliene, 2008; Pineda & Lerner, 2006). The 2010 Gonzales study concluded that leaders should form objective team effectiveness measures. Delgado-Pina, Romero-Martinez, and Gomez-Martinez (2008) identified the problem with operationalizing the construct of team effectiveness rests with distinguishing between the determinant factors and criteria of team effectiveness (Delgado-Pina et al., 2008). An objective team effectiveness measurement tool could be created and used if organizational leaders established a concrete definition of team effectiveness.

The purpose of the 2010 Gonzales Study was to apply quantitative, correlational research to examine if relationships existed among team task interdependence, group emotional competence, and the effectiveness of teams in hospitals. The study could, and should be, replicated to a wider sample to enhance the validation of the findings. The same research questions and hypotheses could be researched within a variant sample. Application of the results of the study will hold a greater significance with a broader study. The constructs of team effectiveness presented with in the 2010 Gonzales study apply to all organizations. Studies replicated within different industries are warranted.

CONCLUSION

Despite a fair amount of literature on team effectiveness, the solution for complex organizations such as hospitals remains insufficient for leaders (Zaccaro, Heinen, & Shuffler, 2009). Results of the 2010 Gonzales Study identified team task interdependence and group emotional competence as having a statistically significant relationship to team effectiveness. The research and findings of the 2010 Gonzales Study extended the knowledge of the constructs of group emotional competence, team task interdependence, and team effectiveness. Multiple opportunities exist for further research using a similar methodology, allowing further expansion of the understanding of team effectiveness.

REFERENCES

Afarjanc, E., Serapinas, D., & Daugvilien?, D. (2008). Employees' impact to quality

management system effectiveness of higher education organization. *Economics & Management*, 158–159.

American Hospital Association. (2007). *Team based turnover reduction.* Retrieved from http://www.aha.org/aha/calendar-event/2007/070925-cecha.html

Amundson, S. J. (2003). *An exploratory study of emotional intelligence, group emotional competence, and effectiveness of healthcare and human service teams* (Doctoral Dissertation). Retrieved from http://proquest.umi.com.ezproxy.apollolibrary.com

Bunderson, J. S. (2003). Team member functional background and involvement in management teams: Direct effects and the moderating role of power centralization. *Academy of Management Journal, 46*(4), 458–474. Retrieved from http://www.jstor.org/stable/30040638

Cantu, C. J. (2007). *Evaluating team effectiveness: Examination of the team assessment tool* (Doctoral dissertation). Retrieved from http://digital.library.unt.edu/ark:/67531/metadc3990/

Cherniss, C. (2001). Emotional intelligence and organizational effectiveness. In C. Cherniss & D. Goleman (Eds.). *The emotionally intelligent workplace* (pp. 3–12). San Francisco, CA: Jossey-Bass.

Clements, D., Dault, M., & Priest, A. (2007). Effective teamwork in healthcare: Research and reality. *Healthcare Papers, 7*, 26–34.

Creswell, J. W. (2005). *Educational research: Planning, conducting, and evaluating quantitative and qualitative research* (2nd ed.). Upper Saddle River, NJ: Pearson.

Delgado-Pina, M. I., Romero-Martinez, A. M., & Gomez-Martinez, L. (2008). Teams in organizations: A review of team effectiveness. *Team Performance Management, 14*(1/2), 7–21. doi: 10.1108/13527590810860177

DeRue, D. S., & Morgenson, F. P. (2007). Stability and change in person-team and person-role fit over time: The effects of growth satisfaction, performance, and general self-efficacy. *Journal of Applied Psychology, 93*(5), 1242–1253. doi: 10.1037/0021–9010.92.5.1242.

Druskat, V. U., Sala, F., & Mount, G. (2006). *Linking emotional intelligence* and performance at work: Current research evidence with individuals and groups. Mahwah, NJ: Lawrence Erlbaum Associates Publishers.

Druskat, V. U., & Wolff, S. B. (1999). The link between emotions and team effectiveness: How teams engage members and build effective task processes. *Academy of Management Proceedings & Membership Directory,* 1–6.

Druskat, V. U., & Wolff, S. B. (2001a). Building the emotional intelligence of groups. *Harvard Business Review, 79*(3), 81–90.

Druskat, V. U., & Wolff, S. B. (2001b). Group emotional intelligence and its influence on group effectiveness. In C. Cherniss & D. Goleman (Eds.). *The emotionally intelligent workplace* (pp. 132–155). San Francisco, CA: Jossey-Bass.

Druskat, V. U., & Wolff, S. B. (2006). *Group Emotional Competence Survey.* Retrieved from http://www.eiconsortium.org/measures/GEC.htm

Edmondson, A. (1999). Psychological safety and learning behavior in different cultures: Inter-and intranational differences. *Journal of Personality and Social Psychology, 81,* 869–885.

Elfenbein, H. A. (2006). Team emotional intelligence: What it can mean and how it can affect performance. In V. U. Druskat, F. Sala, & G. Mount (Eds.), *Linking emotional intelligence and performance at work: Current research evidence with individuals and groups* (pp. 165–184). Mahwah, NJ: Lawrence Erlbaum Associates, Publishers.

Gantt, S. P., & Agazarian, Y. M. (2004). Systems-centered emotional intelligence: Beyond individual systems to organizational systems. *Organizational Analysis, 12*(12), 147–169.

Gilson, L. L., Mathieu, J. E., Shalley, C. E., & Ruddy, T. M. (2005). Creativity and standardization: Complementary or conflicting drivers of team effectiveness? *Academy of Management Journal, 48*(3), 521–531.

Goleman, D., Boyatzis, R., & McKee, A. (2002). The emotional reality of teams. *Journal of Organizational Excellence, 21*(2), 55–65. Retrieved from http://search.ebscohost.com.ezproxy.apollolibrary.com

Goleman, D., & Cherniss, C. (2001). *Emotionally intelligent workplace: How to select for, measure, and improve emotional intelligence in individuals, groups and organizations.* San Francisco, CA: Jossey-Bass.

Gomez-Mejia, L. R., & Balkin, D. B. (2002). *Management* [eBook Collection]. Retrieved from https://ecampus.phoenix.edu/content/eBookLibrary2/content/TOC.aspx?assetMetaId=f077c9b7-4ca2-4708-89e2-d294e4a64a6b&assetDataId=72d3761a-f185–4522-b8ab-27899ff9ee85

Gonzales, R. A. (2010). *Health care team effectiveness: The relationship between team task interdependence and group emotional competence.* (Unpublished doctoral dissertation). University of Phoenix, Phoenix, AZ.

Gully, S. M., Incalcaterra, K. A., Joshi, A., & Beaubien, J. M. (2002). A meta-analysis of team-efficacy, potency, and performance: Interdependence and level of analysis as moderators of observed relationships. *Journal of Applied Psychology, 87*(5), 819–832. doi: 10.1037/0021-9010.87.5.819

Gundlach, M., Zivnuska, S., & Stoner, J. (2006). Understanding the relationship between individualism-collectivism and team performance through an integration of social identity theory and model. *Human Relations 59*(12), 1603–1632. doi: 10.1177/0018726706073193

Hall, R. (2008). *Applied social research: Planning, designing and conducting real-world research.* South Yarra: Palgrave Macmillan.

Harrison, D. A., Price, K. H., Gavin, J. H., & Florey, A. T. (2002). Time, teams and task performance: Changing effects of surface- and deep-level diversity on group functioning. *Academy of Management Journal, 45*(5), 1029–1045.

Hertel, G., Konradt, U., & Orlikowski, B. (2004). Managing distance by interdependence: Goal setting, task interdependence, and tea-based rewards in virtual teams. *European Journal of Work and Organizational Psychology, 13*(1), 1–28. doi: 10.1080/13594320344000228

Hollenbeck, J. R., Ilgen, D. R., Sego, D. J., Hedlund, J., Major, D. A., & Phillips, J. (1995). Multilevel theory of team decision-making: Decision performance in teams incorporating distributed expertise. *Journal of Applied Psychology, 80,* 292–316. doi: 10.1037/0021–9010.80.2.292

Hsu, B. F., Wang, M. L., Chen, W. Y., & Yu, H. Y. (2007, August). Effect of virtualization level on team effectiveness in information and electronic industries: The moderating effect of task characteristics. *Management of Engineering and Technology, 2626*–2632. Retrieved from http://ieeexplore.ieee.org/xpl/freeabs_all.jsp?arnumber=4349597

Johnson, D. W., & Johnson, R. T. (1989). *Cooperation and competition: Theory and research.* Edina, MN: Interaction Book Co.

Jones, S. D., & Shilling, D. J. (2000). *Measuring team performance: A step-by-step, customizable approach for managers, facilitators, and team leaders* [eBook Collections]. Retrieved from https://ecampus.phoenix.edu/content/eBookLibrary2/content/TOC.aspx?assetid=d816a340–2ce2–496e-910e-0e8a7413e30f&assetmetaid=2b1d54de-e031–4812–9c64–940986e8b3df

Kaiser, R. B., Hogan, R., & Craig, S. B. (2008). Leadership and the fate of organizations. *American Psychologist, 63*(2), 96–110. doi: 10.103710003-066X.63.2 96

Kang, H. R., Yang, H. D., & Rowley, C. (2006). Factors in team effectiveness: Cognitive and demographic similarities of software development team members. *Human Relations, 59*(12), 1681–1710. doi: 10.1177/0018726706072891

Katz-Navon, T. Y. (2005). When collective and self-efficacy affect team performance. *Small Group Research, 36*(4), 437–465. doi: 10.1177/1046496405275233

Katzenbach, J. R., & Smith, D. K. (1993a). The discipline of teams. *Harvard Business Review, 71*(2), 111–120.

Katzenbach, J. R., & Smith, D. K. (1993b). *The wisdom of teams: Creating the high performance organization.* Boston, MA: Harvard Business School.

Kavanagh, S., & Cowan, J. (2004). Reducing risk in health-care teams: An overview. *Clinical Governance: An International Journal, 9*(3), 200–204. doi: 10.1108/14777270410552224

Koman, E. S., & Wolff, S. B. (2008). Emotional intelligence competencies in the team and team leader: A multi-level examination of the impact of emotional intelligence on team performance. *Journal of Management Development, 27*(1), 55–75. doi: 10.1108/02621710810840767

Koman, E., Wolff, S. B., & Howard, A. (2007). The cascading impact of culture: Group emotional competence (GEC) as a cultural resource. In R. Emmerling, V. Shanwal, & M. Mandal (Eds.), *Emotional intelligence: Theoretical and cultural perspectives.* San Francisco, CA: Nova Science Publishers.

Kozlowski, S. W. J., & Ilgen, D. R. (2006). Enhancing the effectiveness of work groups

and teams. *Psychological Science in the Public Interest, 7*(3), 77–124. doi: 10.1111/j.1529-1006.2006.00030.x

Liden, R. C., Wayne, S. J., & Bradway, L. K. (1997). Task interdependence as a moderator of the relation between group control and performance. *Human Relations, 50*(2), 169–181. doi: 10.1177/001872679705000204

Leggat, S. G. (2007). Effective healthcare teams require effective team members: Defining teamwork competencies. *BMC Health Services Research, 7*(17). doi: 10.1186/1472-6963-7-17

Mathieu, J. E., Gilson, L. L., & Ruddy, T. M. (2006). Empowerment and team effectiveness: An empirical test of an integrated model. *Journal of Applied Psychology, 91*(1), 97–108. doi: 10.1037/0021-9010.91.1.97

Mathieu, J., Maynard, M. T., Rapp, T., & Gilson, L. (2008). Team effectiveness 1997–2007: A review of recent advancements and a glimpse into the future. *Journal of Management, 34*(3), 410–476. doi: 10.1177/0149206308316061

Mayer, J. D., Salovey, P., & Caruso, D. R. (2004). Emotional intelligence: Theory, findings, and implications. *Psychological Inquiry, 15*(3), 197–215. Retrieved from http://search.ebscohost.com.ezproxy.apollolibrary.com

McCallin, A., & Bamford, A. (2007). Interdisciplinary teamwork: Is the influence of emotional intelligence fully appreciated? *Journal of Nursing Management 15*(4), 386–391.

McShane, S. L., & Von Glinow, M. A. (2005). *Organizational behavior: Emerging*

realities for the workplace revolution. New York, NY: McGraw-Hill Companies, Inc. Nembhard, I. M., & Edmondson, A. C. (2006). Making it safe: The effects of leader inclusiveness and professional status on psychological safety and improvement efforts in health care teams. *Journal of Organizational Behavior, 27*(7), 941–966. doi: 10.1002/job.413

Oatley, K. (2004). Emotional intelligence and the intelligence of emotions. *Psychological Inquiry, 15*(3), 216–222.

Payne, G. T., Benson, G. S., & Finegold, D. (2009). Corporate board attributes, team effectiveness, and financial performance. *Journal of Management Studies, 46*(4), 704–731.

Pineda, R. C., & Lerner, L. D. (2006). Goal attainment, satisfaction, and learning from teamwork. *Team Performance Management, 12*(5/6), 182–191. doi: 10.1108/13527590610687938

Salovey, P., & Mayer, J. D (1990). Emotional intelligence. *Imagination, Cognition, and Personality, 9*(3), 185–211.

Saltman, D. C., O'Dea, N. A., Farmer, J., Veitch, C., Rosen, G., & Kidd, M. R. (2007). Groups or teams in health care: Finding the best fit. *Journal of Evaluation in Clinical Practice, 13*(1), 55–60. doi: 10.1111/j.1365–2753 .2006.00649.x

Shea, G., & Guzzo, R. (1987). Group effectiveness: What really matters? *Sloan Management Review, 28*(3), 25–31.

Staples, D. S., & Webster, J. (2008). Exploring the effects of trust, task interdependence and virtualness on knowledge sharing in teams. *Information Systems Journal, 18*(6), 617–640. doi: 10.1111/j.1365–2575.2007.00244.x

Stubbs, E. C. (2005). *Emotional intelligence competencies in the team and team leader: A multi-level examination of the impact of emotional intelligence on group performance* (Unpublished doctoral dissertation). Western Reserve University, Cleveland, OH.

Takase, M., Maude, P., & Manias, E. (2005). Nurses' job dissatisfaction and turnover intention: Methodological myths and an alternative approach. *Nursing & Health Sciences, 7*(3), 209–217. doi: 10.1111/j.1442-2018 .2005.00232.x

Tata, J., & Prasad, S. (2004). Team self-management, organizational structure, and judgments of team effectiveness. *Journal of Managerial Issues, 16*(2), 232–247.

Thompson J. D. (1967). *Organizations in action.* New York, NY: McGraw-Hill.

Wageman, R. (1995). Interdependence and group effectiveness. *Administrative Science Quarterly, 40*(1), 145–180.

Wolff, S. B. (2006). *Group emotional intelligence (GEI) survey: Technical Manual.*

Retrieved from http://www.eiconsortium.org/measures/GEC.htm

Wolff, S. B., Druskat, V. U., Koman, E. S., & Messer, T. E. (2006). The link between group emotional competence and group effectiveness. In V. U. Druskat, F. Sala, & G. Mount (Eds.), *Linking emotional intelligence and performance at work: Current research evidence with individuals and groups* (pp. 223–242). Mahwah, NJ: Lawrence Erlbaum Associates, Publishers.

Zaccaro, S. J., Heinen, B., & Shuffler, M. (2009). Team leadership and team effectiveness. In E. Salas, G. F., Goodwin, & C. S. Burke (Eds.), *Team effectiveness in complex organization: Cross-disciplinary perspectives and approaches* (pp. 83–112). New York, NY: Psychology Press.

Zeidner, M., Roberts, R. D., & Matthews, G. (2004). The emotional intelligence bandwagon: Too fast to live, too young to die? *Psychological Inquiry, 15*(3), 239–248.

About the Author

Dr. Rachel Ann Gonzales was born in Salt Lake City (SLC), Utah; however, she was very fortunate to have been raised in Kailua-Kona, Hawaii. She moved back to SLC, where she met and married a wonderful man, with whom she now has three boys who she reports are her best accomplishment in life. Dr. Rachel attended undergraduate school at Westminster College obtaining her Bachelors in Nursing. Dr. Rachel's Masters in Nursing (MSN) and Doctorate of Management (DM) were obtained from University of Phoenix. Her doctoral research was on *Health Care Team Effectiveness: The Relationship of Group Emotional Competence and Team Task Interdependence.*

After graduating from Westminster, Dr. Rachel worked as a Home Care Case Manager. She quickly advanced through the ranks of management, serving for a number of years as a Chief Nursing Officer. Currently Dr. Rachel is a Chief Organizational Development Officer/Chief Operations Officer.

Other professional adventures Dr. Rachel has been involved include consulting privately with health care institutions, a professional speaker, President of regional and state nursing organizations, as well as an online professor for University of Phoenix and Capella University.

To contact Dr. Rachel Gonzales, please e-mail cno31012@aol.com

CHAPTER 11

Hiding in Plain Sight:
How Refractive Thinking Found
Three New Independent Variables

Dr. Steven P. Woods

The scientific enterprise as a whole does from time to time
prove useful, open up new territory, display order, and test long-
accepted belief. Nevertheless, *the individual* engaged on a normal
research problem *is almost never doing any one of these things.*
—THOMAS S. KUHN

When I read Kuhn (1996) for the first time, it was as if someone had turned on a brilliant search light. Clearly illumi-
nated against the grey fog of all those years of classes glimmered
the reasons we had been required to take the courses we took,
study the mountain of books, annotate the lifeless articles, and
complete exhausting individual and group assignments. The dissertation check list, the rubrics, the endless minutiae of rules now
looked less irrelevant, even necessary. A sense of gratitude began to
grow for my mentors, sometimes tormentors, who along the way
had required us to study the most influential essay of scientific philosophy ever written. Without this knowledge, it is probable that
the Woods 2009 dissertation *Relationship of Work Related Skills,
Behaviors, and Interests to the Adoption of Web-based Hiring Systems* would have never been written.

This is not to say that this research discovered paradigm-shatter-
ing scientific revelations, but interested readers have found the

results to be valuable. As you will see, in light of the incremental gains in explaining the phenomenon of information technology adoption by seasoned investigators, comparatively speaking, this study by an 'outsider' made a significant contribution to the body of knowledge. In this chapter, I will share how the influence of the Kuhn (1996) essay led me to readily see why a certain invisible college of scientists had become 'stuck' so to speak, in explaining a serious modern-day global problem. In short, my goal for this research summary is to demonstrate that one must first understand why the 'box' is the way it is if we are to think *out-of-the-box,* and then become empowered to *change* the box, which is the essence of refractive thinking and the antecedent to scientific revolution.

WHY WON'T THEY USE IT?

Like many of us, I rarely use *all* the features and capabilities of the vast number of machines and devices I own. This occurs when a certain feature is simply not useful to me or in some cases, is just too hard to use. I fear I will never get my DVD/CD player to play certain song tracks in a certain order from multiple CDs in the player tray.

What I find most curious is situations where an obviously advantageous technology is not adopted by individuals or organizations, particularly information technology (IT). Few would object to the notion that knowledge acquisition and management are crucial to a competitive edge in 21st century enterprises, and IT provides the backbone for knowledge management (Becerra-Fernandez, Gonzalez, & Sabherwal, 2004). Leaders must choose and deploy relevant technologies to derive benefit and maintain market position. Those leaders who fail to adopt and diffuse technologies used by competitors risk their organization's market position and competitive advantage.

Leaders, managers, and information system researchers often

make two assumptions about information technology acceptance and adoption as they seek to implement technologies across organizations. First, IT users who adopt technology will be more productive and produce higher quality products and services; and second, spending in new information technologies will produce an acceptable return on investment (Mahmood & Mann, 2005). In light of my personal experiences and the literature review conducted for the 2009 Woods dissertation, these assumptions proved to be often unrealized.

In several companies where I was an employee and later in my career when providing consulting services, I saw repeated incidents of failures to adopt IT software or systems that clearly would have added to efficiencies and hence, profitability. For example, I have seen countless cases of the purchase of expensive customer relationship management (CRM) software, a powerful tool to retain buyers and very often, only a small percentage of sales employees consistently used the CRM. *Why won't they use CRMs and other information technologies, I asked?* Finding an answer, or at least attempting to find an answer to this question became the central strategy in the journey of my dissertation.

The question of why is worthy of investigation. Organizations in the U.S. spend billions of dollars on IT, yet information system (IS) researchers report a persistent problem of substandard usage levels and below system-capability usage throughout organizations (Jeyaraj, Rottman, & Lacity, 2006). These frequent failures of incomplete IT adoption do not appear to have an effect on buying habits. In fact, IT spending has consistently been on the rise. Consider the following data.

The influential IT research and consulting firm Gartner reported that global IT spending in 2010 was $3.4 trillion, up 5.4% from 2009. In 2011, Gartner expects global IT spending to reach $3.6 trillion, or a 5.7% increase from 2010. By 2015, global IT spending is projected to be well over $4 trillion ("Quarterly IT Spending," 2011). This reality stands in stark relief against continuing IS studies that consistently find that only 20 to 30% of IT projects provide satisfactory outcomes to the organizations that purchase them ("Failure Rate", 2011). Conclusion: *at best this year, over $2.5 trillion will be squandered globally in failed IT adoption.* I imagine there are a number of countries who would be pleased to have a GDP that large.

As I continued to ponder the problem of adoption and non-adoption of IT, I knew my research must be based on and framed in theory. I consider myself a social scientist, a psychologist, and the only theory related to technology I was familiar with was Rogers' (2003) Diffusion of Innovations (DOI) theory, arguably the most researched behavior science theory ever written. Rogers (2003) posited that IT was virtually synonymous with innovation. Thus, I took great interest in what he had to say.

While Rogers' (2003) DOI theory remains a powerful model for explaining a social process and the behaviors it stimulates, by its nature, it is not *predictive.* Having been trained in the traditions of psychology, I knew that cognitive skills, personality traits, and occupational interests are robustly predictive of many behaviors. Psychologists are not typically concerned with the specific determinants of the use of a single technology. Where would I find my theoretical foundation?

I remember clearly the day I noticed a brief footnote in one of the required texts for our studies of knowledge management. There at the bottom of the page in a tiny font, the note read "Much IS research has concentrated on the development of the technology acceptance model (TAM) [Davis, 1989] which identifies two factors associated with user acceptance of information technology to be *perceived usefulness* and *perceived ease of use*" (Becerra-Fernandez et al., 2004, p. 8). Only a fellow doctoral student could understand the excitement I felt at that moment. I had a mature field of research to draw upon. Surely I would find unanswered questions and new work yet to be done as is always the case in major fields of investigation. Then in the next instant I wondered—*Is this another profound grasp of the obvious?*

STRUGGLES IN TAM LAND

TAM researchers have evenly studied adoption of communication IT (email, voice mail, FAX), general purpose systems (Windows, e-commerce, groupware), office systems (word processors, spreadsheet, presentation), and specialized business systems such as hospital telemedicine (Lee, Kozar, & Larsen, 2003). Likert-type surveys with good validity and reliability were most often the vehicles for capturing the data.

It did not take long for me to see that the TAM was the foundation for virtually all of the current research the IS field had done around IT adoption (at that time, current meaning 2004 and up). In the IS community, this 20 year old theory was a mature paradigm and was viewed as the most predictive and parsimonious construct to explain individual IT acceptance and adoption (Lee et al., 2003). However, after reading the first 75 studies, it became clear to me that IS research based on the TAM had struggled for 20 years since Davis (1989) introduced it to understand adoption and non-adoption of useful ITs (Jeyaraj, Rottman, & Lacity, 2006; Lee et al., 2003). Progress by investigators to explain the variables of adoption was incremental, additive, and could be seen to have fairly distinct phases.

With the invention of the printed circuit board and the eventual innovation of 'remote stations' and proliferation the personal computer, researchers in the late 1960s began to ask why usage levels were well below system capabilities. From the very beginning, adoption by individuals of IT was seen as problematic. Research examining dozens of variables continued through the 1970s. Davis (1986) dissertation introduced the TAM providing the IS community a parsimonious model with simple and clear variables. The Davis (1989) study confirmed and elaborated the two independent variables of perception (perceived ease of use, r = 0.45; perceived usefulness, r = 0.63), and the IS community rather quickly rallied around his paradigm. This began what the IS community calls the TAM introduction period. Three other distinct periods would follow.

Lee et al. (2003) suggested that the model introduction period tapered off by 1995, while the model validation period can be thought to have begun in 1992, and ending in 1996. The model extension period is thought to have started in 1994 and lasted until 2003; modest gains had been made in explaining adoption behaviors. With the model elaboration near the beginning of 2000, investigators reached back to include the type of variables not examined since the 1970s. The Zmud (1979) meta-analysis referenced studies throughout the 1970s that examined personality variables such as extroversion/introversion, risk tolerance, and anxiety level among many others. Investigators began to look for independent variables beyond those of user perceptions to personality traits, and cognitive considerations. *FINALLY, I thought!*

Agarwal and Prasad (1998) proposed 'personal innovativeness in the domain of information technology' or PIIT. They defined PIIT as "the willingness of an individual to try out any new information technology" (p. 206). Agarwal and Prasad (1998) conceived innovativeness as a trait, not a belief. This study is notable because it was among the first TAM-based research in nearly a decade to view adoption as a function of a trait, a relatively invariant characteristic of behavior. Agarwal and Prasad (1998) created and validated an instrument to measure PIIT, selected World Wide Web use as the innovation under study, and following validation, tested PIIT on 175 business professionals. The result of their labor was modest: r = 0.47 at p < 0.01 for PITT to explain usage intentions. These investigators went to the trouble of developing an instrument with acceptable reliability and validity to measure the 'innovativeness' of IT adopters. Creating a psychometric instrument (test) is a significant undertaking. *Why didn't they use something off the shelf?*

My psychological training and experience fully grounded me in a belief that human behavior, certainly one as complex as using an IT, can only be explained by examining cognitive skills, behavioral traits, and vocational interests, that is, multiple factors at the same time. While valuable, I felt that the Agarwal and Prasad (1998) PIIT trait provides limited understanding of the complexities of adoption decisions that can include cognitive skills, many other work related traits, and vocational interests. *Why weren't they seeing what I was seeing?*

With the introduction of TAM II (Venkatesh, 2000; Venkatesh & Davis, 2000), the model elaboration period began in earnest. With the introduction of seven independent variables borrowed from other models, the TAM II found perceived ease of use to explain 60% ($R^2 = 0.60$) of usage of an IT, and perceived usefulness to explain 40 to 60% ($R^2 = 0.4$ to 0.6) of usage. Just 3 short years later, the giants of TAM research unveiled UTAUT—the Unified Theory of Acceptance and Use of Technology.

Venkatesh, Morris, Morris, and Davis (2003) proposed four key constructs—performance effort and expectancy, social influence, and facilitating conditions moderated by age, experience, gender, and voluntariness. These collaborators had gleaned their constructs from eight competing models and asserted their model could account for 70% of intentions to use technology, and 50% of actual use. This was good progress, but there was obvious work yet to do.

SHOWDOWN AT THE IS CORRAL

The IS community knew that the once parsimonious and simple TAM had put on a great deal of weight and still was not delivering a solid punch. In the spring of 2007, a special issue of a top tier IS journal, the *Journal of the Association for Information Systems,* invited prominent researchers to express their take on what 20 years of labor had yielded. Even in the formal, stilted style of a peer reviewed journal, you could feel the tension in the room so to speak.

Benbasat and Barki (2007) asserted, "In conclusion, the main thesis of this commentary is that [the] TAM has fulfilled its original purpose and that it is time researchers moved outside its limited confines" (p. 216). Benbasat and Barki (2007) argued that the singular focus on the TAM has distracted researchers from pursuing other important determinates of IT adoption creating illusions of theoretical progress. Further, these investigators posited that researchers have constantly extended or expanded TAM to the point where theoretical chaos reigns because there is no commonly shared adoption model. Goodhue (2007) commenting on Benbasat and Barki (2007) agreed that TAM has been "overworked" (p. 220) and there is a need to go back and look to new directions. Straub and Burton-Jones (2007) argued for more studies of common methods variance bias to avoid making TAM linkages potential methodological artifacts. Schwarz and Chin (2007) asked readers to pause and reflect on our thinking around the notion of 'acceptance' in TAM theory. Rather than encouraging more narrow studies, Schwarz and Chin (2007) suggest there are more gains in looking at broader psychological constructs, which became the goal of my dissertation. "Specifically, we encourage broadening our understanding of IT acceptance toward a wider constellation of behavioral usage and its psychological counterparts" (p. 231). Venkatesh, Davis, and Morris (2007) called for additional research that draws constructs from psychology and organizational behavior. These three men represented the germinal theorist, Davis, and the two most influential and prolific researchers, Venkatesh and Morris. One of the more startling conclusions from the literature review was that to date, they were all but totally ignored. *WHY?*

Perhaps the answer is that because these constructs are parts of paradigms from the 'box' of psychology—not information science; in short, they don't 'fit'. The TAM is essentially about a person's belief or perception that an IT will be easy to use and somehow useful, and this determination always occurs within and as a result of a social process. The TAM was influenced by diffusion of innovation theory (Rogers, 2003), a sociological model. Sociological paradigms are about social processes. Constructs of cognition and personality traits, the focus on individual traits and cognitive decision processes, are foreign to the IS/social theory paradigm. Thus, even revered theorists and researchers were ignored. Refection on the training of scientists may be helpful to a fuller understanding of this puzzling situation.

The training of scientists, who were primarily higher education students typically enrolled in Ph.D. programs, is narrow and theory-based. The goal of this training is to prepare the doctoral student to teach, and most importantly, to conduct research of increasingly complex problems that are succeeding finer details of the paradigm the student has been trained to understand. The problems assigned to the student-scientist "continue to be closely modeled on previous achievements as are the problems that normally occupy him during his subsequent independent scientific career" (Kuhn, 1996, p. 47). In short, the student is trained to understand problems, pieces of a puzzle, through the lens of one theory-based paradigm. However, not all scientists are trained in this fashion.

Students trained in a typical Doctor of Management (DM) program are required to have mastery of interdisciplinary theories of learning and behavior—e.g., psychology, sociology, organizational behavior, information science, philosophy, and especially management and leadership theory. This training emphasizes the application of theory and research to solve pressing social, economic, and organizational problems (University of Maryland University College, 2011; Wasserman & Kram, 2009). Graduates of a DM program are highly trained *scholar-practitioners.*

The DM program and my master's degree training in clinical psychology were no doubt responsible for my early astonishment that the psychological variables leading TAM researchers were recently advocating exploration of had not been seen as obvious candidates for rigorous research from the beginning. Further, I was baffled that the mature constructs from psychology with their very extensive body of research were not used in TAM-based investigations. *Answers to the problem of IT adoption were hiding in plain sight!* "Though many scientists talk easily and well about the particular individual hypotheses that underlie a concrete piece of current research, they are little better than laymen at characterizing the established bases of their field, its legitimate problems and methods" (Kuhn, 1996, p. 47).

The review of the literature (152 sources spanning 40 years of research including 133 peer-reviewed articles, 13 books, 3 Web sites, a technical manual, and reference guide; 81% current research, i.e., < 5 years old) quickly confirmed one of Kuhn's (1996) observations: that in all sciences, the first accepted paradigm is responsible for almost all of the experiments that are easily conducted by researchers. This was certainly the case for the TAM. As Kuhn (1996) would predict, the TAM saw two major successive iterations (TAM II and UTAUT) that added increasingly elaborate methods, esoteric language, idiosyncratic variables and

> refinement of concepts that increasingly lessens their resemblance to their usual common-sense prototypes. That professionalism leads, on the one hand, to an immense restriction of the scientist's vision and to a considerable resistance to paradigm change. The science has become increasingly rigid. (p. 64)

Thus, the answer to my previous *WHY?* is now revealed—*we see what we are trained to see, we do what we are trained to do, and we teach what we were trained to teach.* These observations became the inspiring factors for a research project that would be a radical departure from the well established scientific tradition of the TAM. To a significant degree, this was refractive thinking.

A REFRACTIVE RESEARCH APPROACH

As previously discussed, TAM research has looked at a large number of ITs—everything from email to customer relation management software. I choose a web-based hiring system IT. Web-based hiring systems are common place and consist of software and hardware to administer and score employment assessments using the Internet. These personality tests measure job–person fit and other salient dimensions of potential performance. Employment assessments hold the promise to improve selection, succession, and promotion and their use has steadily increased (Chilton, Hardgrave, & Armstrong, 2005; Michie & Sheehan, 2005; Nye, Do, Drasgow, & Fine, 2008). I have worked with dozens of companies to implement this type of IT and when properly used, they can dramatically increase company performance, and reduce expensive costs like turnover.

As Jeyaraj et al. (2006) and Venkatesh et al. (2007) asserted, innovation diffusion research and IT adoption studies have generated a considerable number of predictive constructs among many investigations in attempts to explain IT acceptance and adoption. Despite the maturity of these research streams, I could find no study looking at the combined factors of cognition, work-related behaviors, and occupational interests on IT adoption and diffusion. *Why would this be important?*

I have established that the use of IT in the workplace is a critical factor of marketplace success in a global economy. There is little debate in the organizational behavior literature and the industrial/ organizational psychology field that people tend to perform better in a job when their cognitive skills, behavioral traits, and occupational/vocational interests fit a given occupation. To *predict* with some accuracy that a person will do well in a job, we must measure all three. The U.S. Department of Labor has been urging employers to assess the *whole person* for over a decade in *Testing and Assessment: An Employer's Guide to Good Practices* (U.S. Department of Labor, 1999). Using information technology can be incidental to a job, or it can be the focus of a job where job-person fit is crucial.

When reading the TAM-based research literature, you occasionally see a connection between the IT and the research subject's occupation. One of the criticisms of TAM research is that it too often involved convenience populations, e.g., college students. It would seem that the TAM research could have been more fruitful if for instance, the subjects for the spreadsheet software study are bookkeepers or accountants for whom this IT represents a critical tool used daily in their profession. On the other hand, in the numerous TAM email studies, we can safely assume that research subject's use of this IT is not central to job-person fit as is spreadsheet software for accounts. In my view, this frequent lack of a connection between the research subject's occupation and the nature of the IT under study is another great weakness of TAM-type research.

From a TAM perspective, my decision to use IT decision makers as research subjects was a radical departure. The TAM-type studies used so-called end users—the majority of studies used college students. No research located during the literature review found a solitary study using decision maker subjects. It seems to me that if you are concerned about shrinking the billions and trillions of wasted dollars spent on unsuccessful IT adoption, that *it might be relevant to look at the people who make the IT decision for the end users in the first place!* The IS community has long understood the correlation of good leadership and IT adoption success (e.g., Armstrong & Sambamurthy, 1999; Howell & Higgins, 1990; Ettlie, Perotti, Joseph, & Cotteleer, 2005). The omission of decision makers in

TAM studies as somehow non-end users is nonsensical and simply cannot be supported.

My objective was rather simple—I wanted to discover within the process of doctoral dissertation if significant differences exist in the cognitive skills, behavioral traits, and occupational interests of two groups of individuals, data that have the potential to predict adoption of a Web-based hiring system. Information regarding IT decision-maker skills, traits, and interests was derived from an established personality assessment, the Profile XT. I have used this employment-selection instrument for years and it has very good reliability and validity. The reader can find a thorough and convincing defense of this assertion in my dissertation.

There were two easily identifiable subject groups: IT decision makers empowered to acquire information technologies who did not adopt a Web-based hiring system that scored a Profile XT assessment and those that did. Study participants only included those decision makers who completed an assessment and met other participant criteria. Thus, I was aware that the sample may be biased toward decision makers who had more positive perceptions of Web-based hiring systems and the Profile XT instrument than decision makers who did not complete an assessment.

I was measuring a binary dependent variable, adoption or non-adoption of a Web-based hiring system, as related to 19 independent variables utilizing a logistic regression for analysis. The 19 independent variables were obtained from the Profile XT assessment, which measures five cognitive skills, nine behavioral traits, and six occupational interests, for a total of 20 mental measures. One of the cognitive skills, thinking style, is a composite of the other four cognitive scales. I did not include the thinking style scale to avoid compromising the null hypothesis. Composite variables might result in multicollinearity, which can cause an increase in standard errors resulting in less accuracy of analysis of the null hypothesis (Miles & Gilbert, 2005).

I selected logistic regression because Hosmer and Lemeshow (2004) asserted that logistic regression is appropriate when studying one binary dependent variable (I'll buy it; I won't buy it) and a set of independent variables. This statistic is popular in market research for obvious purchase related reasons. The next step was figuring out what size the subject group needed to be.

The G*Power power calculation program of Faul, Erdfelder, Lang, and Buchner (2007) indicated that a sample size of 382 was necessary for the 2009 Woods Study given the large group of independent variables and logistic regression statistic. Given the extensive use of the Profile XT instrument for nearly 20 years, random collection of this number of assessments was not a challenge. Within the time allotted for assessment collection, 423 random Profile XT assessments completed by IT decision makers were collected and checked for compliance with several additional criteria for inclusion in the study. Noteworthy is the fact that the Woods (2009) investigation is among the largest research sample groups in IS research history.

With the assessments in hand, the actual research could begin in earnest. A *t* test and logistic regression were the statistical tests to four simple research questions: 1) are the cognitive skill scores 2) behavioral trait scores, and 3) occupational interest scores of decision makers who adopted a Web-based hiring system significantly different from the scores of decision makers who did not adopt a Web-based hiring system? And finally, 4) what is the predictive relationship of Profile XT scale scores and membership in the adopter and nonadopters' groups? The questions get at new and important determinants of IT adoption.

Rogers (2003) contended that when evaluating an innovation, potential adopters seek how-to knowledge and principles knowledge, which are learning behaviors. These thinking and learning behavioral processes tap cognitive skills to reduce risk and form competent decisions about innovation adoption and use. The four cognitive skills measured by the assessment examine "the ability to use old learning applied to new experiences, to measure the flexibility of thinking required to grasp concepts in a job or training setting" (Profiles International, 2006, pp. 2–11) and are applicable and job-related to the requirements of all employees. Information systems researchers have not studied these cognitive variables although there were several calls for their study; it was high time someone did.

Research Question 2 was designed to address the differences in the work-related behaviors of nonadopters and adopters, which is an area of great interest to diffusion of innovation (DOI) and IT adoption researchers (Lee et al., 2003; Rogers, 2003). This is the domain of research we find where 'innovativeness' and PITT are explored. The behavioral scales of the Profile XT provide the foundation for nine behavioral hypotheses and their measures for my dissertation, and no IS research has examined them.

Research Question 3 was designed to address the differences in occupational interests of the two groups, an area that has seen considerable investigation by innovation and IT adoption researchers (Lee et al., 2003). While the studies have been useful in understanding technology adoption, curiously, no IS studies considered the mediating influences of vocational interests associated with person–job fit. The Profile XT's occupational scales show good reliability, validity, and close intercorrelations with other vocational measures (e.g., Holland, 1985). Because these scales measure the full range of occupational interests and potentially provide a rich data set regarding individual differences, inclusion of the six scales seemed essential.

Where differences in the independent variables were found, research Question 4 was designed to discover if a predictive relationship exists between scores of cognitive skills, behavioral traits, and occupational interests of decision makers who adopted and did not adopt a Web-based hiring system. If predictive relationships exist, there is potential to add a new set of constructs toward more effective understanding of IT adoption. This has been the goal of a considerable body of research for many years (Rogers, 2003), and it was my goal too.

WHAT WAS FOUND

Of the 423 assessments randomly collected, slightly more were from adopters of the Web-based hiring system (217 assessments, or 51.3%) than from nonadopters (206, or 48.7%). The response counts to the 19 independent variables were performed first followed by calculating the means for all participants. *Eureka!* The review of the means and standard deviations indicated that certain skills, traits, and interests of adopters of the Web-based hiring system differed from nonadopters. To examine whether significant differences existed in the means, an independent samples *t* test was performed. Nine variables were significantly different (all $p < .05$): numeric reasoning, energy, assertiveness, attitude, decisiveness, accommodating, independence, enterprising, and people service. I knew I was on to something. My long-standing hunch looked like it might hold water.

The *t* tests certainly justified performing a logistic regression. For the logistic regression data to have value, multicollinearity must be assessed and resolved; this analysis showed that 81 out of a possible 171 combinations between the variables, or 47%, had significant correlations with one another. Collinearity statistics were also calculated for each independent variable and the tolerances and variance inflation factor (VIF) results were within acceptable limits.

Because some readers may go on to read the entire study, I want to pause here and provide a word or two about interscale correlations in good psychometric instruments. In short, you *expect* to see these correlations. This can be intuitively understood. Let us say I am high in 'energy', a desire to have lots of balls in the air, to have lots of activity of a different variety going on all the time. One would expect a high energy person to be decisive, and the Profile XT shows an interscale correlation of these two traits at r = .806. Similarly, the research for the Profile XT found the decisiveness and assertiveness scales to be highly correlated (r = .708). "The degree of the intercorrelation between these two scales supports the view that people who are confident and decisive are more likely to express their beliefs to others in a confident manner" (Profiles International, 2006, pp. 3–6). The test publisher, Profiles International (2006) contended that decisiveness is associated with propensities for risk-taking. Energy is associated with working at a fast pace and generating activity and excitement. They are naturally related, so we expect to see these types of interscale correlations.

LOGISTIC REGRESSION FINDINGS—
THREE OUT OF NINETEEN AIN'T SO BAD

The study examined a total of 19 independent variables. Among the four cognitive skills examined, logistic regression showed that numerical reasoning reliably predicted adoption status. The value of the coefficient showed that an increase of one STEN (standard ten) score in numerical reasoning is associated with an increase in the odds of being an adopter by a factor of 1.153 (95% confidence interval: 1.026–1.297). Thus, the results supported rejection of the null hypothesis for the cognitive skill measures.

For the group of nine behavior traits, attitude reliably predicted adoption status. The value of the coefficient showed that an increase of one STEN score in attitude is associated with an increase in the odds of being an adopter by a factor of 1.170 (95% confidence interval: 1.042–1.314). Thus, the results supported rejection of the null hypothesis for the behavior traits group.

Finally, the six occupational interests, people service reliably predicted adoption status. The value of the coefficient for people service shows that a *decrease* of one STEN score is associated with an increase in the odds of being an adopter by a factor of .848 (95% confidence interval: .757–.950). Thus, the results supported rejection of the null hypothesis for the occupational interest group. The table below summarizes these findings.

TABLE 1. *VARIABLES PREDICTING WEB-BASED HIRING SYSTEM ADOPTION*

Variable	B	SE	Wald	df	Sig.	Exp(B)	95% CI for EXP(B) Lower	Upper
Numeric reasoning	.151	.065	5.354	1	.021	1.163	1.023	1.321
Attitude	.157	.061	6.569	1	.010	1.170	1.038	1.319
People service	–.146	.066	4.966	1	.026	.864	.760	.983

Note. CI = confidence interval.

WHAT DID WE LEARN?

I leave it to the reader to decide if the TAM is a bit pedestrian or a robust paradigm. The fact remains that a large group of people have toiled for a long time on a very real and important problem, the effective adoption of information technology. In over 40 years of investigation, IS researchers accounted first for up to 45% of factors of IT adoption, worked steadily adding more and more independent variables (IV) to hit 60% of the variance to adopt, and then at the 20 year mark, to a plateau of 70% supported by many frequently idiosyncratic IVs. In the spring of 2007, foundational and influential investigators alike agreed that the TAM research was in crisis, and investigators needed to take a fresh look at new variables. Then, in the fall of 2009, a naïve researcher (doctoral students are by definition naïve researchers) in just a few months adds three new IVs that explain and additional 12 to 16% of IT adoption, historically, a *substantial* gain. Yes, I was pleased.

"Philosophers of science have repeatedly demonstrated that more than one theoretical construction can always be placed upon a given collection of data" (Kuhn, 1996, p. 76). Kuhn (1996) goes on to explain that this layering of constructions is restricted to the pre-paradigm stage and "very special occasions" (p. 76) during a paradigm's development. Scientists tend to stick with the model they have committed themselves to and the tools it provides to maintain the pace and momentum of discovery. I suggest to the reader that refractive thinking rejects this scientific tradition, this *in-the-box* mentality.

The small achievement of my dissertation was inspired by the work of Kuhn (1996), and enabled by the multidiscipline approach the program creators crafted for my Doctor of Management in Organizational Leadership training. My earlier training in clinical psychology laid much of the foundations of the variables I see when solving problems in organizations. I have always felt that these two disparate training programs have provided me a very powerful set of lenses to see the world in different ways than traditional training provides, that is to provide me the opportunity to be a *refractive thinker.*

Limitations of time and space prevent me from discussing suggestions of how I believe the TAM community might build upon my contribution to IT adoption, so I must save those for another day. This essay opened with a quote from Kuhn (1996) asserting that normal (traditional) science will almost never "prove useful, open up new territory, display order, or test long accepted belief" (p. 38). *I submit that refractive thinking provides opportunities to break the mold of normal science and contribute new knowledge to solve everyday problems.* To my fellow learners and in conclusion—may we all think outside of the box so that we may *think refractive* to *change* the box, as we learn and share our paradigms.

REFERENCES

Agarwal, R., & Prasad, J. (1998). A conceptual and operational definition of personal innovativeness in the domain of information technology. *Information Systems Research, 9*(2).

Armstrong, C. P., & Sambamurthy, V. (1999). Information assimilation in firms: The influence of leadership and IT infrastructures. *Information Systems Research, 10*(4), 304–327.

Benbasat, I., & Barki, H. (2007). Quo vadis, TAM? *Journal of the Association for Information Systems, 8*(4), 211–218.

Chilton, M. A., Hardgrave, B. C., & Armstrong, D. J. (2005). Person-job cognitive style fit for software developers: The effect on strain and performance. *Journal of Management Information Systems, 22*, 193–226.

Davis, F.D. (1986). *Technology acceptance model for empirically testing new end-user information systems theory and results.* Unpublished doctoral dissertation, MIT, Cambridge. Retrieved from http://hdl.handle.net/1721.1/15192

Davis, F. D. (1989). Perceived usefulness, perceived ease of use, and user acceptance of information technology. *MIS Quarterly, 13*, 319–340.

Ettlie, J. E, Perotti, V. J., Joseph, D. A., & Cotteleer, M. J. (2005). Strategic predictors of successful enterprise system deployment. *International Journal of Operations & Production Management, 25*(9/10), 953–972.

Faul, F., Erdfelder, E., Lang, A.-G., & Buchner, A. (2007). G*Power 3: A flexible statistical power analysis program for the social, behavioral, and biomedical sciences. *Behavior Research Methods, 39*, 175–191. Retrieved from http://www.firthunands.com/Gpower3.pdf

Failure rate: Statistics over IT projects failure rate. (2011). *IT Cortex.* Retrieved from http://www.it-cortex.com/Stat_Failure_Rate.htm

Gartner. (2011, March 29). *Quarterly IT spending forecast.* Retrieved from http://www.gartner.com/technology/research/quarterly-it-forecast/

Holland, J. L. (1985). *Making vocational choices: A theory of vocational personalities and work environments.* Odessa, FL: Psychological Assessment Resources.

Hosmer, D. W., & Lemeshow, S. (2004). *Applied logistic regression: Textbook and solutions manual.* New York, NY: Wiley-Interscience.

Howell, J. M., & Higgins, C.A. (1990). Champions of technological innovation. *Administrative Science Quarterly, 35*(2), 317–342.

IT Budgets: 35% of CFOs say their IT spending will rise moderately this year. (2008). *Controller's Report, 2008*, 14–15.

Jeyaraj, A., Rottman, J. W., & Lacity, M. C. (2006). A review of the predictors, linkages, and biases in IT innovation adoption research. Journal of Information Technology, 21, 1–23.

Kuhn, T. S. (1996). *The structure of scientific revolutions* (3rd ed.). Chicago, IL: The University of Chicago Press.

Lee, Y., Kozar, K. A., & Larsen, K. R. T. (2003). The technology acceptance model: Past, present, and future. *Communications of AIS, 2003*(12), 752–780.

Mahmood, M. A., & Mann, G. J. (2005). Information technology investments and organizational productivity and performance: An empirical investigation. *Journal of Organizational Computing and Electronic Commerce, 15*(3), 185–202.

Michie, J., & Sheehan, M. (2005). Business strategy, human resources, labour market flexibility and competitive advantage. *International Journal of Human Resource Management, 16*, 445–464.

Nye, C. D., Do, B.-R., Drasgow, F., & Fine, S. (2008). Two-step testing in employee selection: Is score inflation a problem? *International Journal of Selection & Assessment, 16*, 112–120.

Profiles International, Inc. (2006). *Profile XT technical manual.* Waco, TX: Author.

Rogers, E. M. (2003). *Diffusion of innovations* (5th ed.). New York, NY: Free Press.

Schwarz, A., & Chin, W. (2007). Looking forward: Toward an understanding of the nature and definition of IT acceptance. Journal of the Association for Information Systems, 8(4), 230–243.

Straub, D. W., & Burton-Jones, A. (2007). Veni, vidi, vici: Breaking the TAM logjam. *Journal of the Association for Information Systems, 8*(4), 223–229.

U.S. Department of Labor, Employment and Training Administration (1999). *Testing and assessment: An employer's guide to good practices.* Retrieved from U.S. Department of Labor web site at http://wdr.doleta.gov/research/FullText_Documents/99%2Dtestassess%2Epdf

Venkatesh, V. (2000). Determinants of perceived ease of use integrating control, intrinsic motivation, and emotion into the technology acceptance model. *Information Systems Research 11*, 342–365.

Venkatesh, V., Davis, F. D., & Morris, M. G. (2007). Dead or alive? The development, trajectory and future of technology adoption research. *Journal of the Association for Information Systems, 8*(4), 267–286.

Venkatesh, V., Morris, M. G., Davis, G. B., & Davis, F. D. (2003). User acceptance of information technology: Toward a unified view. *MIS Quarterly, 27*, 425–478.

University of Maryland University College, 2011. *Frequently Asked Questions Doctor of Management Program*. Retrieved from http://www.umuc.edu/programs/grad/dm/dmfaq.shtml#14

Wasserman, I. C., & Kram, K. E. (2009). Enacting the scholar-practioner role: An exploration of narratives. *The Journal of Applied Behavioral Science, 45* (1), 12–38.

Woods, S.P. (2009). *Relationship of work related skills, behaviors, and interests to the adoption of web-based hiring systems*. (Unpublished doctoral dissertation). University of Phoenix, Phoenix, AZ.

About the Author

Dr. Steven P. Woods is an accomplished entrepreneur, intrapreneure, and management professor who brings over 40 years of executive experience in the government, non-profit, and for-profit sectors into his classrooms. Dr. Woods is an engaging, passionate assistant professor at the Merrick School of Business, University of Baltimore, where he teaches entrepreneurship, organizational behavior, global management, human resource management, and operations management. He is Chair, Academic Affairs Committee for the Advisory Board of the Entrepreneurial Opportunity Center, and a member of Undergraduate Program Committee.

In addition, Dr. Steve acts as the faculty advisor for all management-related internships, and the *Leadership UB* leadership certificate program at the Rosenberg Center for Student Involvement. Professor Woods holds the degrees of Doctor of Management (DM) in Organizational Leadership from University of Phoenix, a MA in clinical psychology, and a BA in developmental psychology both from Antioch University.

A self-described serial entrepreneur, Dr. Steve founded his consulting firm, Workforce Metrics, in 2001, and today the firm primarily serves small and medium sized clients from the east coast to Alaska. Workforce Metrics provides out-of-the-box solutions to complex organizational dynamics. To many clients, Dr. Steve is their *Company Doctor*.

Dr. Steve is a die-hard Baltimore Ravens football fan and spends his free time jamming with friends (rock, blues, some folk and country), gardening, and showing his two grandchildren how people never really do grow up.

For more information about Dr. Steve, please contact swoods@ubalt.edu

The Refractive Thinker®: The Future of Innovative Thought

Dr. Cheryl A. Lentz

OUR MISSION STATEMENT

The purpose of The Refractive Thinker® is to facilitate the publishing needs of doctoral scholars while collaboratively sharing the expense and the promotion.

As *The Refractive Thinker® Doctoral Anthology* series moves forward, questions continue to surface regarding the concept of refractive thinking itself. These include: what is a refractive thinker®, how did the concept of refractive thinking begin, and what value does this add to the concept of *thinking* and *critical thinking?* This commentary provides an in-depth analysis of this dynamic perspective as we continue to expand our definition of the elusive refractive thinker. This volume continues this mission of this power project of discovery.

WHO IS A REFRACTIVE THINKER®?

First, let us begin our discussion with the concept of *refractive thinking* itself. This concept emerged when I concluded the concept of critical thinking was incomplete. Having taught this for more than 10 years, there is more than simply an either or dichotomy where if thinking is *inside* the box, and critical thinking is *outside* the box. What then is beyond this approach? Who are those among us that think beyond this dichotomy? Enter the refractive thinker.

A refractive thinker is someone that is insatiable with their curiosity. They are not satisfied within current conventional parameters or the prevailing wisdom. They are frustrated by provincial thinking or analysis. They do not follow the crowd. Instead, the crowd follows *them*. They ask questions as they continue to dig deep in their pursuit of knowledge and understanding. They do not excel within the constraints of only an either/or option where many believe there are only two options: *in the box* or *out of the box* boundaries. Instead of merely preferring to color outside of the lines, they prefer to redefine the very rules that constrain the lines themselves, questioning the very structure itself.

Refractive thinkers are often those individuals innovating new business models, those who make new scientific discoveries, and those who offer never before held theories to try explaining existing or new phenomenon. They are the explorers of thoughts, those who are willing to ask the right questions that often take them—and those following them—in new and unchartered waters. The refractive thinker is comfortable with limitless boundaries and the suspensions of rules. Refractive thinkers are the pioneers such as Sir Isaac Newton, Albert Einstein, Benjamin Franklin, Leonardo da Vinci, Mohandas Gandhi, and Madame Curie to name but a few. They are those that not only ask *why,* but *why not.*

HOW DID REFRACTIVE THINKING BEGIN?

To quell that persistent voice in the back of my mind and to think beyond self-imposed restrictions, *The Refractive Thinker®: Volume V: Strategy in Innovation* offered the genesis for refractive thinking. In the interest of brevity, the short version is the frustration I felt in struggling with the participants in the seminar who were insistent on trying to put old ideas into old structures. For the first

3 days of what was intended to be expansive brainstorming, we could not advance as a group. Why? In reply this lack of progress, I offered us permission to think *beyond* boundaries, to learn to tolerate ambiguity without form, to believe in the process and allow the shape to evolve on its own. This was an amazing experience where the energy simply shifted at that one very moment in time. Voila— refractive thinking was born.

Once I took the rules and *perceived* limitations away, and gave everyone permission to allow *the situation* to dictates its form, our creativity generated an expansive array of new ideas. A new path emerged. As in the words of Peter Senge (1990), we cannot put new ideas into old constructs.

HOW DOES REFRACTIVE THINKING BENEFIT STUDENTS AND EMPLOYEES?

Individuals within either academia or the business landscape seem to find comfort with what they currently regard as truth. To reiterate, refractive thinking is *beyond perceived* limits of the proverbial box.

The design looks toward existing issues and opportunities while suspending judgment, freeing one's mind to be limitless. Refractive thinking goes beyond the rules, simply existing where one suspends and resists any type of confinement, labels, or parameters of any kind. This free thinking without any convention at all is something that few truly can obtain.

Einstein was one of the rare few who could think beyond that had not been previously considered. He strove to decipher behavior in a way that did not follow conventional wisdom. Initially, few could grasp the radically different concepts Einstein put forth. Much like during the time of Sir Isaac Newton or perhaps even further when the earth was believed to once be flat, these are the pioneers who represent the ideals of refractive thinking.

Descartes offers the often quoted phrase: *"I think therefore I am."* Allow me to expand this view by adding "I critically think *to be,* I refractively think *to change the world"* (Lentz, 2009). My goal is to help adult learners develop their critical thinking skills to see what is already there through a slightly different lens. This new perspective enables them to learn to question everything they see-and to have their curiosity drive them to question, *why.*

Refractive thinking embraces the post modernism guise of being able to hold divergent points of view and theory *simultaneously.* It builds a foundation of duality. Society is uncomfortable with simultaneous duality—the thought that two divergent boundaries can exist and both can be correct—*from their point of view* is challenging to wrap one's arms around. Dealing within not only duality but multiplicity of meaning is where refractive thinking exists, expands, and offers a new contemplation of thought. The goal is to be able to simply exist within a modality of asking *why* and *why not,* to suggest *what if?* The goal is to build the capacity to understanding limitlessness.

What is it that prevents most people from achieving this state? Why is it easier to cling to the safety of the confines of the proverbial box allowing only the dichotomy of opposites, or either or extremes? Instead, why not break this cycle of fear and simply stop? Perhaps the solution is not a box *at all.* Instead, this is a free form that is fluid and dynamic. Can we exist without having to clearly define the parameters of that existence? This is the quest of the refractive thinker®—to discover the yet unknown and to realize that one cannot put new ideas into old constructs (Senge, 1990).

About the Editor

Southern Nevadan internationally published author Dr. Cheryl A. Lentz holds several accredited degrees; a Bachelor of Arts (BA) from the University of Illinois, Urbana-Champaign; a Master of Science in International Relations (MSIR) from Troy University; and a Doctorate of Management (DM) in Organizational Leadership from University of Phoenix School of Advanced Studies.

Dr. Cheryl, affectionately known as 'Doc C' to her students, is a university professor on faculty with Colorado State University-Global, Embry-Riddle University, University of Phoenix, The University of the Rockies, and Walden University. Dr. Cheryl serves as a dissertation committee member, faculty mentor, is a dissertation coach and also offers expertise in editing in APA style for graduate thesis and doctoral dissertations. She has earned her Sloan C Certification from Colorado State University—Global as well as her Quality Matters Peer Reviewer (APP/PRC) Certification.

Dr. Cheryl is also an active member of Alpha Sigma Alpha Sorority.

Additional published works include her dissertation: *Strategic Decision Making in Organizational Performance: A Quantitative Study of Employee Inclusiveness, The Golden Palace Theory of Management, Journey Outside the Golden Palace, The Refractive Thinker®: Vol. I: An Anthology of Doctoral Learners, Vol. II: Research Methodology, Vol. III. Change Management, Volume IV: Ethics, Leadership, and Globalization,* and *Volume V: Strategy in Innovation.* For additional details, please visit her website: http://www.drcheryllentz.com

To reach Dr. Cheryl Lentz for information on any of these topics, please e-mail: drcheryllentz@gmail.com

Index

A
Andragogy, 3

B
Breckenridge, 91, 94, 101, 109
Business ethics, 36, 44
Business performance, 35, 54, 57

C
CAM therapies, 100, 101–104
Case history, 2, 21
Character, 2, 18, 21, 25–26, 36, 39,
40, 44, 45, 48, 53–57, 63, 78, 98,
111, 119–121, 139, 154, 197,
214, 218
Complementary therapies, 90–93,
95–98, 100, 101, 104
Comparative analysis, 40, 133, 139,
149
Content analysis, 63, 78, 82, 133,
136–138, 140–141, 143,
145–147, 149–155
CMMI, 134–136, 140–142, 145,
149–154
Cross case, 3, 8, 10, 134
Culture, 3, 6, 7, 35–50, 52, 53,
55–57, 102, 122, 172

D
Data collection, 5, 9–11, 17, 24–28,
45, 47–50, 57, 70, 78–80, 96,
103, 117, 136, 143, 144,
149,160, 162, 164, 166, 173,
178, 179, 191, 192
Data management, 10
Decision-making, 36, 65, 73, 97, 151,
155
Descriptive statistics, 136, 137, 139,
146
Diffusion of innovation, 212, 217,
223

E
Ethnography, 5, 6, 9, 11, 36, 38–43,
46, 48–50
Exploratory, 52, 80, 82, 116, 121,
133, 136, 137, 177

H
Healing, 90–93, 95, 97, 100, 108
Holistic, 1, 6, 50, 52, 63, 65, 82,
89–91, 94, 95, 102, 103, 105,
134, 155

I
Innovative qualitative multiple case
study, 17, 30
Information technology (IT), 45, 135,
210
Intrinsic, 3, 35, 122

L
Leadership, 44, 55, 56, 63–65, 72–78,
82, 83, 89, 91, 92, 96, 104, 109

Other Books by
THE REFRACTIVE THINKER® PRESS

The Refractive Thinker®: Volume I: An Anthology of Higher Learning

The Refractive Thinker®: Volume II: Research Methodology

The Refractive Thinker®: Volume III: Change Management

The Refractive Thinker®: Volume IV: Ethics, Leadership, and Globalization

The Refractive Thinker®: Volume V: Strategy in Innovation

Available in e-book, Kindle®, Ipad®, Nook®, and Sony e-Reader, as well as individual e-chapters by author.

Coming Fall 2011

The Refractive Thinker®: Volume VI: Post Secondary Education

Telephone orders: Call us at 877 298-5172

Fax Orders: Fax us at 877 298-5172

Email Orders: info@refractivethinker.com

Website orders: Please place orders through our website:
www.refractivethinker.com

Postal Orders: The Refractive Thinker® Press
9065 Big Plantation Avenue
Las Vegas, NV 89143-5440   USA

Refractive
Thinker®
Press

The Refractive Thinker®: Volume I:
An Anthology of Higher Learning

The title of this book, *The Refractive Thinker*®, was chosen intentionally to highlight the ability of these doctoral scholars to bend thought, to converge its very essence on the ability to obliquely pass through the perspective of another. The goal is to ask and ponder the right questions; to dare to think differently, to find new applications within unique and cutting-edge dimensions, ultimately to lead where others may follow or to risk forging perhaps a new path entirely.

The Refractive Thinker®: Volume II:
Research Methodology

As in Volume I, the authors within these pages are on a mission to change the world, never satisfied or quite content with what is or asking *why*, instead these authors intentionally strive to push and test the limits to ask *why not*. *The Refractive Thinker*® is an intimate expression of who we are—the ability to think beyond the traditional boundaries of thinking and critical thinking. Instead of mere reflection and evaluation, one challenges the very boundaries of the constructs itself.

For more information, please visit our website: www.refractivethinker.com

from The Refractive Thinker® Press

The Refractive Thinker®: Volume III: Change Management

This next offering shares yet another glimpse into the scholarly works of these authors, specifically on the topic of change management. In addition to exploring various aspects of change management, the purpose of *The Refractive Thinker®* is also to serve the tenets of leadership. Leadership is not simply a concept outside of the self, but comes from within, defining our very essence; where the search to define leadership becomes our personal journey not yet a finite destination.

The Refractive Thinker®: Volume IV: Ethics, Leadership, and Globalization

The purpose of this next volume in *The Refractive Thinker®* series is to share yet another glimpse into the scholarly works of these authors, specifically on the topics of ethics, leadership, and concerns within the global landscape of business. I invite you to join with me as we venture forward to showcase the authors of Volume IV, and continue to celebrate the accomplishments of these doctoral scholars affiliated with many phenomenal institutions of higher learning.

For more information, please visit our website: www.refractivethinker.com

Please send the following books:

- ❏ *The Refractive Thinker®: Volume I:*
  An Anthology of Higher Learning
- ❏ *The Refractive Thinker®: Volume II:*
  Research Methodology
- ❏ *The Refractive Thinker®: Volume II:*
  Research Methodology, 2nd Edition
- ❏ *The Refractive Thinker®: Volume III:*
  Change Management
- ❏ *The Refractive Thinker®: Volume IV:*
  Ethics, Leadership, and Globalization
- ❏ *The Refractive Thinker®: Volume V:*
  Strategy in Innovation

Please contact the Refractive Thinker® Press for book prices, e-book prices, and shipping.
Individual e-chapters available by author: $3.95 (plus applicable tax).   www.refractivethinker.com

Please send more FREE information:

- ❏ Speaking Engagements
- ❏ The Refractive Thinker® Press Educational Seminars
- ❏ Consulting

Join our Mailing List

Name:_____

Address: _____

City: _____ State: _____ Zip: _____

Telephone: _____ Email: _____

Sales tax: NV Residents please add 8.1% sales tax

Shipping: *Please see our website for shipping rates.*

Refractive
Thinker®
Press

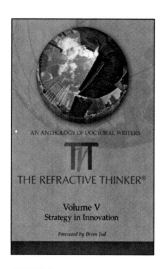

Please send the following books:

❏ *The Refractive Thinker®: Volume I:*
   An Anthology of Higher Learning

❏ *The Refractive Thinker®: Volume II:*
   Research Methodology

❏ *The Refractive Thinker®: Volume II:*
   Research Methodology, 2nd Edition

❏ *The Refractive Thinker®: Volume III:*
   Change Management

❏ *The Refractive Thinker®: Volume IV:*
   Ethics, Leadership, and Globalization

❏ *The Refractive Thinker®: Volume V:*
   Strategy in Innovation

Please contact the Refractive Thinker® Press for book prices, e-book prices, and shipping.
Individual e-chapters available by author: $3.95 (plus applicable tax).   www.refractivethinker.com

Please send more FREE information:

❏ Speaking Engagements

❏ The Refractive Thinker® Press Educational Seminars

❏ Consulting

Join our Mailing List

Name:_____

Address: _____

City: _____ State: _____ Zip: _____

Telephone: _____ Email: _____

Sales tax: NV Residents please add 8.1% sales tax

Shipping: *Please see our website for shipping rates.*

Refractive
Thinker®
Press

Participation in
Future Volumes of
The Refractive Thinker®

Yes I would like to participate in:

❑ **Doctoral Volume**(s) for a specific university or your organization:

Name: _____

Contact Person: _____

Telephone: _____ E-mail: _____

❑ **Specialized Volume**(s) Business or Themed:

Name: _____

Contact Person: _____

Telephone: _____ E-mail: _____

Please mail or fax form to:

The Refractive Thinker® Press
9065 Big Plantation Ave.
Las Vegas, NV 89143-5440 USA

Fax: 877-298-5172
www.refractivethinker.com